PRAISE FOR
PAID ATTENTION

'A new marketing philosophy for our time.'
Ben Richards, Global Chief Strategy Officer, Ogilvy & Mather

'The most over-asked question by five-year-olds is the most under-asked questions by adults – "why?" Why do we do things this way? Why do we make certain assumptions? Why don't we try a different method? Faris steps into the role of advertising's irritating toddler in an effort to understand why the industry is in the state it's in and what it can do to regain its relevance. Faris asks the questions the rest of the ad industry are too scared to ask. And now that he's done it, it'll be interesting to see which agencies will make the changes the rest of the industry will be too scared to make. Here lie the nuggets of wisdom you'll hear repeated in ad agency board rooms for years to come. Take a read, collect some quotes and sound like the smartest person in the room before someone else does.'
Dave Birss, Editor at Large, *The Drum*

'In the digital age and beyond, marketers can no longer buy attention. That means how we define strategy, creative ideas, media, and even the role of the consumer has to change. Faris Yakob has spent a career writing and speaking about these topics. Few thinkers better understand the challenges that confront marketers, advertisers and agencies in the years to come. Finally, we have his knowledge – captured in a clear, logical text that offers readers an understanding of the recent changes, and what we can do to prosper. Traditionalists will resist much of what Faris Yakob has to say in *Paid Attention*. But they do so at their peril. Faris has laid out a convincing argument for why and how marketers and agencies need to change in an age when media is abundant and attention is scarce. I, for one, am paying attention.'
Edward Boches, Professor of Advertising, Boston University. Former Partner and Chief Creative Officer, Mullen

'*Paid Attention* is a must-read for anyone struggling to understand media's changing relationship with consumers in a world being transformed by digital. Funny and provocative, and packed full of great examples, it'll get you thinking differently, whether you're an advertising professional or a media entrepreneur trying to reposition your business to take on the next generation of opportunities.'
David Flynn, Chief Creative Officer, Endemol UK

'Ever been on a roller coaster? – they tend to hold your attention well. Slowly scaling great heights, then wonderful views, sharp unexpected turns, fast paced, and great fun. Faris' book is a roller coaster of a book, full of ideas on ideas, it held my attention at every turn. Packed full of theories and evidence to weigh and consider, this is the advertising/communications/ideas book of the year.'
Adam Ferrier, Chief Strategy Officer, Cummins & Partners and author of *The Advertising Effect*

'A lively, penetrating, thoroughly intelligent investigation of how content wins attention... or fails to do so. Let Faris be your guide to new ideas and best practice.'
Grant McCracken, affiliate Berkman Center for Internet & Society at Harvard University and author of *Chief Culture Officer* and *Culturematic*

'Faris manages to eloquently encapsulate the ongoing radical transformations of marketing and communication as a practice. From behavioural sciences to the genesis of creativity, this book keeps on travelling between both sides of our brains in view to intelligently explain the productive tension between arts and sciences, and the recent shift towards a less intuitive, thus more evidence-based scientific approach to marketing... without, importantly, killing creativity, but *au contraire*, enhancing it by rendering ideas more relevant and efficient.'
Christophe Cauvy, Regional Director of Digital & Innovation (Europe), JWT

'In today's global, 24/7, hyper-connected environment, our attention is the most prized commodity. New media call for new approaches to strategic communication. Drawing upon a rich and highly interdisciplinary body of scholarship on the links between cognition, symbolic expression and behaviour, *Paid Attention* is a primer for the praxis of persuasion in the 21st century. Clearly fluent in both academic research and marketplace realities, Faris Yakob offers a welcome bridge between theory and practice. Scholars and professional communicators alike should pay attention.'
Gwenyth Jackaway, PhD, Associate Professor and Associate Chair of Communication and Media Studies, Lincoln Center, Fordham University

'Great ideas happen when you ask a lot of questions. If you want to ignite culture, you need to challenge conventions. Faris is one of the brightest and most curious minds in advertising, and in *Paid Attention* he asks questions that every advertiser and marketer should be asking themselves today about breaking through in an increasingly on-demand and attention-scarce world. In the process, he arrives at some revealing brand tactics and strategies. Recommended reading for anyone in the advertising and marketing business.'
Winston Binch, Partner and Chief Digital Officer, Deutsch LA

'This fantastic book will challenge how you think and view the world – it also happens to be incredibly useful for anyone who wants to understand the current and future direction of advertising. Faris takes us on a journey through communications theory, neuroscience, and the history of media, and leaves us with practical and actionable ideas on how to do better work. An absolute must-read!'
David Passiak, Head of Innovation and Research, Dubizzle, and author of *Disruption Revolution*

'Great ideas, as the book explains, are borrowed bits of other great ideas recombined in new and interesting ways. *Paid Attention* doesn't just explain the concept, it lives it, combining ideas from economics, psychology, philosophy, media studies, and, of course, advertising, into a coherent narrative for this particularly incoherent time. The book is well worth your attention and you're sure to find a few ideas to steal for yourself and your brand.'
Noah Brier, founder of Percolate

'Faris Yakob, you most certainly have my attention. But, then again as one of my most valued advisors in this world of communication and creator of the LIA NEW Category, you always have always made me pay attention. What a marvellous read. Intentionally or unintentionally, you have put into perspective the way all media are converging with one another and share similar methods for success, despite which platform they come from or how content is now consumed. Brilliantly, you examine how crucial it is to distribute your work in order to achieve your goals. It is incredible how the concepts, like sharing, which were learned as toddlers in the sandbox, are now the governing rules for a fruitful, profitable campaign. I know this book will be the gold standard for understanding modern concepts about media. But then again, technology changes so quickly, that by the time you finish reading my review, this book will need to be amended in your enviable style. A MUST-read for anyone living in this world of infinite content. I really Paid Attention to every single word.'

Barbara Levy, President, London International Advertising Awards

'The brand communications playbook has changed little in the last century. I think it's safe to say the world we live in has changed dramatically in that time. *Paid Attention* is a hugely useful playbook to draw from in order to develop communications for the world today, not the world of yesterday.'

Gareth Kay, co-founder, Chapter. Former CSO, GS&P

'*Paid Attention* gives a comprehensive view of how the advertising industry has evolved and how new technologies and social media have affected what people demand from brands today. Faris covers philosophy, psychology, behavioural economics and social behaviours to look at how planners and creatives can ensure their work is relevant, engaging and appropriate. He covers a great deal of information in an approachable and straightforward way, with stacks of recent examples of successful advertising.'

Emily Hare, Managing Editor, *Contagious*

'Reading this book felt a little like intellectual pinball as I was bounced between the worlds of psychology, philosophy, economics and advertising history: always entertaining while also sometimes genuinely profound. At a time when almost every pundit seems to be questioning whether advertising has a future, Faris is offering some answers.'

Will Collin, founding Partner, Naked Communications

'Sometimes, reflecting on a broken mirror is a fascinating thing. When chaos disrupts the perception of order it can offer a fresh perspective and jarring insights. Faris brings indisputable advertising credibility to the fluid timeline of the now. The ongoing polemic of conversation in advertising and the precision and force of his thought, against an ever changing context, not only makes *Paid Attention* a powerful read, but a necessary one for any practitioner in marketing today and likely for years to come. I'm not usually one for grand pronouncements, but this could be the most important "tool" I equip myself with for a very long time.'

Michael Kasprow, Partner and Director of Innovation, Union Creative, Toronto

'Faris's phaser is set to stun as he reverses the polarity of the ad industry in a cautionary tale against old media thinking. Salvation comes in the form of numerous helpful thought starters for those genuinely interested in exploring the future of marketing.'

Johnny Vulkan, founding Partner, Anomaly, www.anomaly.com

'We don't think of it this way, but advertising is an industry with a history of its own, shaped by heroes, epiphanies, disasters and luck. It's not often analysed like other industries, but in his book, Faris has laid out a rich and intricate landscape that not only frames the state of advertising today, but the events that contributed to it, and how advertising should evolve in the face of that fast-arriving future we've heard so much about. Grab a thesaurus and get ready for a Billy Madison-esque learning montage.'
Amber Finlay, Director of Communications Planning, Converse

'Faris has hosted sessions for my students on our many trips to New York. His passion and particular lexicon have both challenged and inspired students from around the globe. His new book is about the now and treats digital as the norm that it has become. Unusually for this genre of book, it is light of touch, eminently readable and seamlessly integrates different cultures so as not to appear out of the US. Philosophy, yes in part, but with the common touch.'
Bruce Sinclair, Principal Lecturer, Bucks Adschool, Bucks New University

'Faris is one of the smartest people working in marketing and communications, anywhere in the world. This book will only enhance his reputation further. It is a door into his thinking, a door which reveals the breadth of his thinking and the practicality of his answers to "so what should you do differently?" A joy to read – and not just once. I predict it'll be one of those books we come back to again and again. There are few people today who've thought so deeply about communication and marketing as Faris Yakob. Fewer still who've examined the big issues of the day from such a broad set of perspectives – digging around in the best evidence the industry has produced as well as looking outside to what's happening in technology, in leading-edge cognitive and social science. If you want to fast-track your thinking about what's next and what you need to do about it, this book is for you. And if that doesn't convince you, remember: your competitors will be devouring it, so maybe you should have a look, too!'
Mark Earls, The Herdmeister, author of *HERD*, *I'll Have What She's Having*, and *Welcome to the Creative Age*

Paid **Attention**

Innovative advertising for a digital world

Faris Yakob

KoganPage

LONDON PHILADELPHIA NEW DELHI

Publisher's note

Every possible effort has been made to ensure that the information contained in this book is accurate at the time of going to press, and the publishers and author cannot accept responsibility for any errors or omissions, however caused. No responsibility for loss or damage occasioned to any person acting, or refraining from action, as a result of the material in this publication can be accepted by the editor, the publisher or the author.

First published in Great Britain and the United States in 2015 by Kogan Page Limited

Apart from any fair dealing for the purposes of research or private study, or criticism or review, as permitted under the Copyright, Designs and Patents Act 1988, this publication may only be reproduced, stored or transmitted, in any form or by any means, with the prior permission in writing of the publishers, or in the case of reprographic reproduction in accordance with the terms and licences issued by the CLA. Enquiries concerning reproduction outside these terms should be sent to the publishers at the undermentioned addresses:

2nd Floor, 45 Gee Street	1518 Walnut Street, Suite 1100	4737/23 Ansari Road
London EC1V 3RS	Philadelphia PA 19102	Daryaganj
United Kingdom	USA	New Delhi 110002
www.koganpage.com		India

© Faris Yakob, 2015

The right of Faris Yakob to be identified as the author of this work has been asserted by him in accordance with the Copyright, Designs and Patents Act 1988.

ISBN   978 0 7494 7360 0
E-ISBN   978 0 7494 7361 7

British Library Cataloguing-in-Publication Data

A CIP record for this book is available from the British Library.

Library of Congress Cataloging-in-Publication Data

Yakob, Faris.
   Paid attention : innovative advertising for a digital world / Faris Yakob. – 1st Edition.
      pages cm
   ISBN 978-0-7494-7360-0 (paperback) – ISBN 978-0-7494-7361-7 (ebk)   1. Advertising.
2. Branding (Marketing)   3. Electronic commerce.   I. Title.
   HF5823.Y335 2015
   659.1–dc23
                                                                           2015000915

Typeset by Graphicraft Limited, Hong Kong
Print production managed by Jellyfish
Printed and bound by CPI Group (UK) Ltd, Croydon, CR0 4YY

CONTENTS

11   Prospection: Planning for the future we want   156

Epilogue: Talkin' about your generation   170

LIST OF TOOLKITS

The above toolkits are available to download in pdf format at:
www.koganpage.com/PaidAttention

ABOUT THE AUTHOR

Faris is co-founder of the strategy and innovation consultancy Genius Steals, built on the belief that ideas are new combinations (and everything else mentioned in this book). Genius Steals is itinerant, working with brands, agencies and start-ups all over the world. Being nomads allows Faris and his wife and partner Rosie to go to wherever clients need them and to be inspired by the world in between.

Previously he was founding partner of creative technology boutique Spies&Assassins, chief innovation officer of MDC Partners, and EVP chief technology strategist at McCann Erickson NYC. Before that he worked as digital ninja at Naked Communications, in London and Sydney. Faris has variously been a communication strategist, media planner, account planner, creative director, a writer for *Maxim* magazine and a management consultant.

He has won and judged numerous advertising awards. He chaired the Content&Contact and Integrated categories at the Clio awards and helped to create the NEW category for the London International awards. He consulted on, and briefly featured in, *The Greatest Movie Ever Sold* (2011) by Morgan Spurlock.

Faris speaks at events all over the world, and tries very hard not to bore audiences, because, like Kurt Vonnegut, he believes one should 'use the time of a total stranger in such a way that he or she will not feel the time was wasted'.

He received an MA in English Literature and Language from Lady Margaret Hall College, Oxford.

He is a contributing author to *Digital State*: *How the internet changes everything* (2013) and *What is a 21st Century Brand?* (2015), published by Kogan Page. He was named one of ten modern-day Mad Men by Fast Company but hopes he is less morally bankrupt than the television show characters.

Despite living on the road, you can reliably find him on Twitter (@Faris) and on his blog: **www.farisyakob.com.** For more information on Genius Steals head to **www.geniussteals.co.**

He likes nice people to get in touch and he hopes you have a very lovely day.

THANKS!

Writing a book takes a lot longer than you think. At least it did for me. So the amount of people who have helped me along the way is truly innumerable. Inevitably, some of you reading this will have helped me inestimably and will not see your names below. I'm very sorry about that. I really, really appreciate everything you did.

Thanks, then, in no particular order, to:

My wife Rosie Yakob, for being my partner in mind, business, life and adventures. I could never have dreamed of starting our company or finishing this or doing anything that we have done together without you. Thank you for being patient with me. Especially as I was writing this whilst we were setting up a company whilst planning a wedding whilst living on the road.

My parents, who only ever asked me to find something and someone that would make me happy, and supported me in every twist and turn of my circuitous career. No, Dad, I don't have a job, I have a company now. No, I'm not cutting my dreadlocks off. Yes, Mum, I am still travelling.

To my brothers, Laith and Ramzi, whose brilliance drives me even if I don't see them and their families as often as I would like.

To everyone who has been kind enough to host us as we travel, especially as I've been writing. My parents, Natalya, Sibilla and Aran and Max, Judy and Erik, Lillian and Jason, Scott and Teresa, Adrian and Philippa, Antonia and Ronan, Elmo, both of 'the Rachels', and every other gracious, generous host.

To my best men, Andrew Jackson, Ben Richards, Dave Shnaps and Neil Mendoza, who have all inspired me more than they know.

To everyone who pointed out when they think I'm wrong. To the haters that made me strong.

To Polly, Paul, Marion and Mel, for keeping me sane. To all my drinking companions for companioning me.

To Henry Jenkins, whose book inspired me to write, and who inspired me to teach.

To every blogger from 'back in the day' who helped me hone my thinking. To my mentors, especially the Naked Boys (Will Collin, Ivan Pollard, Jon Wilkins, Adam Ferrier) and Nick Kendall, whose IPA Excellence Diploma got me started on this path nearly a decade ago.

To all the planners who are helping craft the craft and make the work *work*.

To all the young people I've got to work with or speak to over the years who decided they wanted to spend their spare time learning on courses I was making up, and for inspiring me to be less cynical.

To my editor, Anna Moss, who helped shape these rough-hewn words into a book-like object.

To my assistant, Merritt Decloux, for her tireless assistance, especially with the many pages of endnotes.

To our clients, past, present and future, for believing in us and for being lovely.

And finally, of course, to you gentle reader, without whom this book doesn't really exist.

Rock ON.

PART ONE
Paid attention

Introduction
Paid attention – how much is it worth?

> *Friends, Romans, countrymen, lend me your ears.*
>
> *JULIUS CAESAR*, WILLIAM SHAKESPEARE[1]

Are you paying attention to the attention being paid for? For the entirety of its history, the media industrial complex has been aggregating human attention in order to sell this attention to advertisers. Indeed, broadcast mass media was conceived *as* advertising, since radio stations were initially set up in order to encourage the sale of radio sets. Back then anyone could buy and run a local radio transmitter. My wife's grandfather went into business with a local tyre dealer, who was broadcasting from his store when they weren't serving customers. This eventually evolved into a licensed radio station, KWTO, and then into the world's first syndicated music television show, the Ozark Mountain Jubilee. So, initially, the quality of content was spotty at best. In the late 1920s the first national radio broadcasts began in the United States and were quickly commercialized by the newly formed National Broadcast Company and Columbia Broadcast Service. Around the same time, innovations in manufacturing and distribution meant that consumer goods companies could sell their products all over the country, where their reputations had not yet travelled, which left them seeking a way to reach people all over the country with the same messages. The media industry as we now know it was born.

On these first radio stations, and later on television, the primary content was advertising. Individual sponsors supported each show and products were integrated within, leading to *Pabst Blue Ribbon Bouts* and the *Camel Newsreel*. Shows were created by advertising agencies for the brands. This model was inefficient for broadcasters, who could make more money selling slices of attention to multiple sponsors, and challenging for sponsors and their agencies. The economics of content production became prohibitive as budgets skyrocketed an average of 500 per cent between 1949 and 1952.[2] Thirty seconds of airtime was far more affordable to fill than 60 minutes. Interruptive, 'spot' advertising became (and remains) the dominant form, an idea lifted from magazine advertisements that literally interrupt the flow of content to present an advertisement on the page.

The word advertising is derived from the Latin *advetere*, which means to draw attention to something (literally, to turn towards). Since the emergence of interruption, the way advertising drew attention was by paying for attention aggregated by something else. Companies pay for your attention, and hope you are actually paying attention. The amount of money spent buying attention? This is $142.5 billion in the United States alone and $467 billion globally.[3]

Media = bandwidth

All media, in totality, can be understood as the world's total available bandwidth. Analogue broadcasting grew linearly, as new media were invented and techniques refined. Digital encoding allowed for far greater compression but more importantly made media an aspect of digital technology, which accelerates exponentially.

At the same time, the tools of content creation began to be democratized by the same drivers: professional tools found their way into the hands of the public because their prices dropped and they became easier to use. One defining aspect of technology is how it shifts the locus of intelligence, in waves, from expert individuals, into objects and software that can be used by everyone. What once required a knowledge of code, design, film-editing software and so on, was now possible with basic computer skills.

Blogger, launching in 2003, allowed anyone to publish things directly to the web without any knowledge of HTML. A decade later, Instagram filters let people with no knowledge of photography, film or Photoshop create striking images. A rush of new cultural producers filled the available media space being created. By 2010, according to Google chief executive officer (CEO) Eric Schmidt, mankind was creating as much content every two days as it had from the dawn of civilization up until 2003.[4] This is something in the region of five exabytes of data (an exabyte is 1 billion gigabytes) and this number will continue to accelerate.

So we shifted, rapidly, from a media environment defined by scarcity to one defined by abundance, creating a generation that, as media author Clay Shirky has pointed out, 'have never known a world with only three television channels, a world where the only choice a viewer had in the early evening was which white man was going to read them the news in English'.[5]

Content became digital and ubiquitous and this led to the idea of an *attention economy*. Content is now abundant but the human attention that can be allocated to it is finite. Since the resource being allocated is attention, and economics is the study of the allocation of scarce resources, economic thinking began to be applied to the idea of attention.

Of course, the total amount of content in the world has long dwarfed any individual's ability to consume it. Thinkers from times as diverse as Aristotle, Da Vinci, Milton and Leibniz have all been credited as the 'last man to have read everything'. Today, the variety and pervasive presence of media presents the sense of an ever more fragmented body of knowledge; an ever more fragmented, though global, culture.

As technology investor Esther Dyson has observed:

This attention economy is not the intention economy beloved of vendors, who grab consumers' attention in order to sell them something. Rather, attention here has its own intrinsic, non-monetizable value. The attention economy is one in which people spend their personal time attracting others' attention, whether by designing creative avatars, posting pithy comments, or accumulating 'likes' for their cat photos.[6]

And that means less attention for the advertisers who are paying for it.

According to recent studies, 8- to 18-year-olds are consuming more than seven hours of media a day and, perhaps unsurprisingly, are consuming multiple media concurrently.[7] (It would be hard to understand how they find time for school otherwise.) The proliferation of personal screens that is evident everywhere, and the possibilities suggested by augmented reality devices such as Google Glass, a head-mounted display that projects a screen into the user's field of view, have led some to suggest that we may soon reach the peak levels of attention available.

We live immersed in media. Anyone who is trying to get the public to notice something – whether a commercial exhortation, health message, political appeal, or to promote their own cause or skills – offers content to which they hope their intended audience will pay attention. While the media industrial complex often still attracts the largest amounts of attention, it is now in competition with content from brands, and every Tweet, Facebook post, picture and video, on YouTube, Instagram or Vine (the six-second video mobile phone application from Twitter) made by other people. It is perhaps little wonder that attention deficit disorder (ADD; also known as ADHD, attention deficit hyperactivity disorder) is one of the most salient psychological conditions, or at least concerns, of our time: diagnoses of ADHD have risen by 66 per cent since 2000.[8] It has even been suggested that the 'average American attention span' is declining because of the internet.[9]

Communication is persuasion

Effecting change is an inherent function of all communication, be-cause communication is persuasion. In 1948 communication theorist Harold Lasswell described communication as having five parts:

Who (says) What (to) Whom (in) What Channel (with) What Effect.

Channel is now used interchangeably with medium but back then channel referred to a sense, so television, the *medium*, would use both the audio and visual *channel*.

The communications industry concerns itself with a specific subset of communication. Communication in its broadest sense can be defined as any means by which 'one mind may affect another'.[10] Commercial communication can be described as the dispersion of persuasive symbols and messages to manage mass opinion, from logos to advertising. However, this persuasion element is embedded in the notion of communication.

Humans have an in-built desire to spread their own ideas. There are compelling anthropological reasons for this. We pass on our ideas in order 'to create people whose minds think like ours',[11] because this delivers an evolutionary advantage: there is safety in numbers.

Any time we communicate anything to anyone, we are attempting to change the way their brains operate. We are attempting to change their view of the world, so that it more closely resembles our own. Every assertion, from the notion of a deity to giving someone directions, attempts to harmonize the receiver's beliefs about the world with the transmitter's.

The objectives of commercial communications are to influence mass opinion and behaviour, usually purchase behaviour, increasing purchase frequency and volume, or increasing price inelasticity of demand. Due to the cost involved in buying attention and creating content, the most efficient drivers of change constitute more successful ideas. These ideas are increasingly spread by their recipients, influencing more behaviour as they go, ultimately creating a multiple on the impact of media exposure and providing the brand with a competitive advantage.

Ideas grow, thrive and effect change in proportion to the amount of attention allocated to them. They function like solidarity goods – a class of economic goods 'whose value increases as the number of people enjoying them increases'.[12] These ideas could be knowledge of the qualities of certain plants, religions, brands, legends, scientific principles such as evolution, political dogma, fashion trends, misguided beliefs about sex, rumours, gossip, philosophy, jokes and so on. Ideas that get allocated a lot of attention tend to survive, although in recent times rapid spikes in attention are often followed by corresponding nadirs.

The oldest and most successful idea in history provides a perfect example of how ideas worked in a linguistic culture. The principle of reciprocity, also known as the golden rule, is a fundamental moral tenet found in all major religions in almost exactly the same form: 'Treat others as you would like to be treated.'[13] It is highly generative since it can be used in almost any decision and, as the foundation underlying every major religion, it is difficult to envisage a more potent agent of behavioural change.

Similar to many of the ideas that have existed for thousands of years, the golden rule is aphoristic, expressed in a concise and memorable form. Proverbs are the oldest class of successful ideas, nuggets of wisdom that transcend centuries and cultures. For example, versions of the proverb 'where's there's smoke, there's fire' have appeared in more than 55 languages.[14] The success of these ideas is driven partially by function and partially by form.

Ideas that are allocated no attention at all – those that are never exposed to anyone – make no impact on the world, by logical extension, since no one sees them. The 50 per cent of YouTube videos with less than 500 views don't individually make much impact on culture.[15]

So attention is a powerful thing – but what kind of thing is it?

Attention is like water

Attention is like water. It flows. It's liquid. You create channels to divert it, and you hope that it flows the right way.[16]

APOLLO ROBBINS, PICKPOCKET/ILLUSIONIST

Buying attention is a way to appear inside an existing channel that has diverted attention. (Yet another way of using *channel*. Or is it the same?)

Like many psychological phenomena, attention is usually understood subjectively. Its nature can be hard to pin down, like the related idea of consciousness. For example, attention seems to have both directionality and a normative duration – if it didn't then a disorder based on its deficit wouldn't make sense – but the specifics are blurry. The psychological present is estimated to be about three seconds long,[17] but a three-second attention span would not be considered normal so we must be able to string these psychological 'nows' together into contiguous sequences.

One of the classic definitions of attention comes from William James, one of the progenitors of modern psychology, in his book *The Principles of Psychology*:

> Everyone knows what attention is. It is the taking possession by the mind, in clear and vivid form, of one out of what seem several simultaneously possible objects or trains of thought. Focalization, concentration, of consciousness are of its essence. It implies withdrawal from some things in order to deal effectively with others.[18]

As James's appeal to common knowledge suggests, attention could only be analysed through introspection. Modern neuroscience can show us which areas of the brain need more oxygen when we are paying attention and this has already demonstrated that 'attention' is made up of a number of different cognitive processes.

You can pay attention to something voluntarily, or you can have it snatched away by an explosion, or someone speaking your name across a crowded room (the so-called *cocktail party effect*). You can stare right at something, which is overt attention, and you can pretend not to while still focusing on it, which is covert. Attention is socially directed, which is to say you can draw someone's attention to something by focusing your gaze on it, which is known as joint attention. Most importantly, you have a limited capacity for attention, which restricts how much information you can derive from sensory stimulus at a time:

> When you attend to something, it is as if your mind aims a spotlight onto it. You actively ignore virtually everything else that is happening around your spotlight, giving you a kind of tunnel vision.[19]

This leads to the phenomenon of *inattentional* blindness, where you fail to notice something that is fully visible because your attention has been directed elsewhere. It is here that concerns may lie about whether someone watching the advertisements on television is really seeing them. It is also closely related to *change blindness*, where you do not notice a change in scene when your attention is taken from it for an instant. One of the overwhelming features of our perception, and counter-intuitive to our experience of it, is how limited it actually is. We don't *actually see* a lot of what we are looking at, but the brain fills in these gaps all the time, both in what we see and what we remember, in what is known as *fabulation*.

This slippery property, attention, is of incredible and increasing value. Since it follows logically that ideas that are allocated no attention can have no impact (although, as we will see, this is not entirely so, because of the different kinds of ettention), attention is therefore considered a prerequisite for effecting any change through communication. It is enshrined in the earliest, and still dominant, cognitive model for advertising: AIDA:

A – Attention: the prospective customer's attention is attracted.

I – Interest: the interest in that product is raised.

D – Desire: some of these prospects begin to desire the thing.

A – Action: they then do something about it, such as buying it from a shop.

Since some people are 'lost' at each level (less people will be interested than see it and so on) this gave rise to the idea of a 'purchase funnel', where one seeks to garner as much attention as possible, as you lose a certain percentage of prospects at each stage thereafter. Thus the traditional formulation of advertising was understood to be the process of buying the most attention of the largest number of the desired audience at the lowest possible cost. The cognitive cascade that followed was assumed to lead to people buying things.

This endless filling of a mythical funnel created the media industrial complex and the prevalence of advertising we have in culture today, an ever-escalating race to drown out the utterances of others, and garner the most attention. In light of the dramatic changes to the market for ideas, this model has begun to be supplemented, and in some cases superseded, by a subtle transition. Instead of paying professional media companies for attention, what if companies – and indeed individuals – could earn it for themselves?

The rest of the book

In a particularly vigorous online discussion of something I wrote, an anonymous commenter (aren't they always!) accused me of being an 'advertising philosopher'. Although it was meant as an insult, suggesting my concerns were ephemeral not practical, I rather liked it. Whilst I don't claim to be a philosopher, this book nonetheless aspires to be a modern philosophy of advertising – a set of beliefs that guide behaviour. Philosophy is both theory *and* praxis.

In the rest of the book we will look at how brands operate and innovate in the evolving market for ideas. We will consider:

- What kind of ideas brands are and how they have established themselves in the attention niche left by myth.
- How much of the decision-making process happens below the threshold of attention.
- How advertising uses attention and how it works best in a dynamic attention market.
- A guide to what ideas are and how to have them.
- How to behave in this new world of infinite content.
- How to package ideas to attract the most attention in the advertising industry.
- How strategy is evolving to reflect these changes.

Still paying attention? Then let's go.

Logocentrism
What's in a name?

The great idea in advertising... is in the realm of myth.

LEO BOGART[1]

It is perhaps surprising that, in an age when Procter & Gamble (P&G) is willing to spend US $57 billion buying Gillette, and McKinsey can state that 'intangible assets make up most of the value of M&A deals [and that] brands account for a considerable portion of these assets',[2] there is such a degree of uncertainty as to what is being purchased.

Uberconsultant Tom Peters has proclaimed that we are in 'The Great Age of the Brand'.[3] Yet if you ask Google, the oracle of said age, it pulls up dozens of different definitions of brand, ranging from 'trade name: a name given to a product or service' to 'the personality of an organization' or 'the symbolic embodiment of all the information connected with a product or service'. The 'Great Age of the Brand' would seem to be an age of great uncertainty.

Things were not always this complex. Brands used to be simple, as any cowboy (or cow) could have told you. But society has evolved at a remarkable pace in the last century and brands have evolved with them. Brands seem to chase our own needs up Maslow's hierarchy: from badge of origin to transformative experience. What was a signifier of product quality can now be shorthand for a service, an experience, a 'sign of me',[4] a celebrity, a country and you, gentle reader.[5] Brands are everywhere and everything is a brand. We live in a logocentric world.

Brands are the most recognizable and ubiquitous cultural force operating today. Children are named after them,[6] and their encroachment on public space is detailed with gleeful vitriol in books such as

No Logo (1999) by Naomi Klein. Brands are reference points we use to define ourselves ('I am irresistible, I say, as I put on my designer fragrance... I am a juvenile lout, I say, as I down a glass of extra strong lager: I am handsome, I say, as I don my Levi jeans'[7]) and identify other people ('Only chavs wear Burberry'[8]). Our comprehension of these meanings 'demonstrates the rise to prominence of the brand in the last century'.[9] How are we to resolve this contradiction – that as brand influence has grown, what brands are has become less certain?

The apparent confusion is a function of the nature of the role that brands now play. I believe that brands perform the role of myths in modern society and therefore must be complex. Even the simplest brands, which seem to provide only origin information or navigation assistance on the shelf, have multiple constituent parts. Their nature reflects their ability to capture attention.

We are 'meaning-seeking creatures'.[10] We have imagination and this leads us to wonder about the larger context in which we exist. This can lead us into existential despair, and since the beginning of human culture we have constructed stories that place us in a larger setting, and thus give us the sense that our lives have meaning. 'Reality leaves a lot to the imagination', to quote John Lennon. These stories resolve the contradictions between different types of human experience, providing our lives with a meta-narrative to explain them that is integral to all human societies. This role is now performed by brands, which 'enable us to make sense and create meanings for ourselves in the social world of consumption in which we participate'.[11] Brands are 'ideas to live by',[12] which we look for due to our 'tradition hunger'.[13]

The emergence of brands as myths has been triggered by the decline of standard myths in Western culture. This is also why brands began in the West, and are spreading East, as the adherence to mythology as an organizing principle is breaking down. Western modernity is 'the child of *logos*'[14] (the opposite of *mythos* in the Hellenistic tradition, it represents science and facts). Science became the dominant paradigm for understanding the world. But *logos* alone is unable to give us a sense of significance – it was myth that gave life meaning and context. Thus society unconsciously cried out for and ultimately created its own myths around the newly dominant force of consumerism, allocating disproportionate amounts of attention to the ones that best filled these needs. This is why modern brands are more complex than their older counterparts, because the role of brands is changing to fulfil the need for, the evolutionary niche left by, myth. *Logos* led us to logos.

The most powerful of today's brands developed a cohesive mythology. Brands in the modern world are inseparable from the companies whose 'soul' they manifest: Larry Page and Sergey Brin from Stanford, vowing that Google would not be evil; Innocent Drinks's cute packaging and grass-covered vans; the baristas/partners at Starbucks – these are all elements of the brand that are held together by a philosophy that guides behaviour. This combination of narrative and values is myth.

Myths are inherently complex and polysemous; they can be interpreted in a number of equally valid ways. They cannot be compressed into a single, particular essence but are rather the sum total of interlinked elements. Thus, brands cannot simply represent a single core value. Claude Lévi-Strauss (the anthropologist, not to be confused with the founder of the denim brand) called the constituent parts of a myth *mythemes*. He argued that myth is a language of its own, not just a subset of language, as it can be broken down and restructured, irrespective of the language it is delivered in.

I would argue that brands are a language of their own, expressed via word or image or sound, via television or print or mouth. Brands are a bundle of inextricable, irreducible parts we can call *brandemes*.

Coca-Cola is not *just* about happiness. Its brandemes might be redness; youth; Father Christmas; sharing; the liquid; the shape of the bottle; 'the Real Thing'; new/classic versus Pepsi; teaching the world to sing; and many other connected ideas. Some of us will only engage with some of these meanings. Like myths, we apply interpretation; we construct the meaning for ourselves – and this flexibility is crucial, increasingly so in the global brand marketplace. This is what allows so many different iterations of a brand to all hold true. The story of the myth is distinct from its form:

> That story is special, because it survives any and all translations.
> Lévi-Strauss says that myth can be translated, paraphrased, reduced,
> expanded, and otherwise manipulated – without losing its basic shape
> or structure.[15]

Lévi-Strauss posited that: 'it is likely that languages exist in which an entire myth can be expressed in a single word'.[16] There is – the language of brand.

Myths are constructed in a space that is both real and imagined, where reality is magical and the impossible is real. They are experienced ritually, via purchase or use or interaction with brand communication, which provides a bridge to the brand's domain.

Holt suggests that we 'buy the product to consume the myth'.[17] I agree, but would argue that brands are not the icons of myth, but the myth itself (the logo is not the brand), and that any interaction with brand communication can function in a similar way. The Marlboro man lives in Marlboro country, but this can no longer be directly communicated, since tobacco advertising has been banned in much of the world. Marlboro therefore created 'installations' in bars, with red sofas in front of video screens showing scenes that evoke Marlboro country.[18] Whilst this may not feel ethical, it is designed to provide subliminal access to an established, mythic, brand space.

The *brand* brand is itself a myth. This is why it is so hard to pin to a definition, because many definitions are true and make up, collectively, what the brand myth is. They are the brandemes of *brand*. And the *brand* brand helps to resolve the contradiction between influence and clarity that we observed at the outset: the function of myth is to 'provide a logical model capable of overcoming a contradiction'.[19] Brands are both dominant and vague, because the things humans look to for meaning must be open to interpretation, to allow them to resonate with everyone individually.

The theory of brand/myth leads to a number of new ways of thinking. It suggests that we must abandon the reductionism that attempts to hone brands to a single point and instead embrace complexity. We have to leave our onions and look for guiding principles that connect the brandemes. It suggests we should look to develop meaning and narrative in communications.

There are a number of parallels between advertising and literature.[20] This is because literature is the expression of stories, as advertising is the expression of brand. Stories have characters, events, settings, beginnings, middles and ends, styles, subtexts, twists and turns – and each episode should leave the audience wanting more. This is how we should also think about constructing communication; conceptually and over time.

The launch campaign for mobile brand 3 (UK) demonstrated this well: each ad shows us more of Planet 3 (setting); the Critters (characters) are locked in unending comic battle (plot) that exists at the peripheries of the Japanese 'reality' of the brand ads; there was even a website where you could visit Planet 3 yourself.[21] It helped to drive the brand from a standing start to a major player in a crowded category.

One marketer who was cognizant of crafting a myth is Phil Knight, the founder of Nike. Naomi Klein accuses Nike of 'creating a corporate mythology powerful enough to infuse meaning into... raw objects'[22] – and it has. Here's how a young man explained his decision to get the Nike 'swoosh' logo tattooed over his navel: 'I wake up every morning... look down at the symbol, and that pumps me up for the day. It's to remind me every day what I have to do, which is, "Just Do It".'[23]

CASE STUDY

Google has become the world's biggest brand,[24] without using any traditional advertising (until their first television commercial in the 2012 Super Bowl). Casual observers often maintain that Google built a better mousetrap, that their superior search results naturally drew them users and positioned them as smarter and faster.

This disregards the skill with which the Google myth was constructed. In tests, Google rarely outperforms other search engines. The 2012 Bing campaign, BingItOn, highlights the fact that the Microsoft search engine seems to outperform Google in blind tests. According to their research, people choose Bing web search results over Google nearly '2 to 1 in blind comparison tests'.[25] Yet this seems to make very little difference to Google's market share, which is actually increasing.

One of the core constituents of Google's myth – one of its *brandemes* – is 'being smarter': built on its founders' frozen PhDs, its name,[26] its adoption by the geek community and a careful seeding strategy. Google has always stated a clear developer origin story, which makes it empathetic to geeks – and geeks are the early adopters and cultural disseminators of the internet.

The young hero takes on the might of the evil empire – a classic myth. Google's stark homepage made the implicit statement that they weren't in it for the money, in contrast to all the cluttered portals of the time. They cemented this by running the site for years without monetizing it, building the brandeme of benevolence – 'Don't be Evil'.[27] Its logo can change daily – eventually codified as the Google Doodle – and yet still be Google, because the brandeme isn't the look of the letters, it's the fact that it can change.

It uses products like episodes, unleashing them to a fan base in carefully staged instalments. In 2004 it launched Gmail on 1 April, which generated endless PR. Gmail also fostered the mythic positioning of Google as Skywalker against Microsoft's Evil Empire: it offered 1GB of storage for free, whereas Hotmail was charging for anything over 10MB. Earth, Maps, Drive, Glass, Inbox, even the abandoned Wave – each episode has its own facets and staging. Demonstrating a clear understanding of Knight's maxim that 'product is the most important marketing tool',[28] Google releases products to build its myth.

Modern brands have evolved to fulfil the role of myths for modern consumers, the role of soul for modern corporations – and it is incumbent on the advertising industry to evolve with them.

Brands are socially constructed ideas

The definition of a brand used most often is Paul Feldwick's, the former sage of advertising agency DDB:

A brand is simply a collection of perceptions in the mind of the consumer.[29]

This is great because it reminds us that:

Brands... are made and owned by people... by the public... by consumers.[30]

This definition is part of the orthodoxy of advertising. It also led to a conceptual rift between two kinds of brand equity – that which exists in someone's head and that which can exist on balance sheets as a form of intangible asset.

I don't think this definition is entirely adequate. And I think, with a slight reformulation, we might also be able to begin to resolve the division between brands in our heads and brands that have a dollar value to accountants. In the next few lines following the above quote in the article 'Posh Spice and Persil', Bullmore points out:

> The image of a brand is a subjective thing. No two people, however similar, hold precisely the same view of the same brand.[31]

And of course this is absolutely true. And yet it is also not true. My image of a particular brand will be subjective and yet it will exist in relation to an understanding of the collective perception of the brand. Wittgenstein argued that there is no such thing as a private language. A language that is unintelligible to anyone but its originating user is logically incoherent: it couldn't function as a communication medium, there would be no way for a speaker to assign meanings to its signs.[32]

Equally, an individual brand makes no sense. My understanding of any brand exists in relation to the collective understanding of the brand. That collective intentionality dictates what the brand means – it assigns a type of status function to a product. I may personally disagree but I know what I'm disagreeing with – the collective perception. Brands can only exist if there is a collective perception of what they stand for.

This is what allows brands to be used in defining, or constructing, an identity. If all that mattered is what I personally thought about the brand, it would be unable to perform any social functions at all.

So, let's put forward a reformulation:

A brand is a collective perception in the minds of consumers.

But how does this help to resolve the division between brands in the head and brands on the balance sheet? Because by making it a collective perception, we can turn a brand from an opinion into a fact.

Here I'm going to steal from the philosopher John Searle, who wrote about the construction of social reality. In essence, he argues that, collectively, subjective opinions can create objective reality.

This seems counter-intuitive: how can everyone thinking something make it real?

But in fact we do it all the time. The best example is money. Money is only money because we all agree that it is. Its status as money is not in any way derived from the physical qualities of the note and it is no longer linked to a gold standard. Most money nowadays exists as magnetic impressions on hard drives, but that doesn't matter as long as it functions as money. As long as it can be used to pay debts, it is money – objectively.

If I go into a shop and buy something with some cash, my belief in its value is no longer required, it simply is *money*. This also can be seen to apply to government, property, political parties, wars. All these things only exist because we think about them in a certain way – and yet they do exist.

Similarly, a brand is a form of socially constructed reality that has attained an objective reality, which is why it can have a monetary value that is dependent on the totality of perceptions held about it – the total amount of attention that has been allocated to it.

How much is that brand in the window?

Beyond purchases and goodwill on balance sheets, there are various industry reports that measure the dollar value of the ideas we call brands. The BrandZ report by research company Millward Brown is one of the most respected, but most share a basic methodology compounded with some proprietary data.

The BrandZ valuation uses discounted cash-flow analysis. This is the sum of all future earnings attributable to the brand discounted to account for risk over time. This is pretty standard accounting stuff, but, as with all financial modelling, if you look closely, it is basically certain opinions, assumptions and predictions, structured into a spreadsheet.

The 'brand multiple', for example, is derived using the proprietary *brand voltage* metric, which 'takes into account how many people are very loyal to the brand (the brand's bonding score) and claimed purchasing data for the category to produce a single Brand Voltage number'.[33] This means asking lots of people what they claim to do and then using it to guess what they will do in the future, which, as we shall see, is not a very reliable predictor.

The final formula is this:[34]

Brand value =

Step 1 – intangible earnings: intangible corporate earnings allocated to each brand, based on company and analyst reports, industry studies, revenue estimates, etc.

Multiplied by:

Step 2 – brand contribution: portion of intangible earnings attributable to brand. This is driven by the BrandDynamics Loyalty Pyramid and category segmentation, part of brand voltage study.

Multiplied by:

Step 3 – brand multiple: brand earnings multiple. Calculated based on market valuations, brand growth potential and voltage, the proprietary metric.

The most recent study indicates that the most valuable brands in the world are:[35]

1 Google – $158,843,000,000

2 Apple – $147,880,000,000

3 IBM – $107,541,000,000

4 Microsoft – $90,185,000,000

5 McDonald's – $85,706,000,000

6 Coca-Cola – $80,683,000,000

7 Visa – $79,197,000,000

8 AT&T – $77,883,000,000

9 Marlboro – $67,341,000,000

10 Amazon – $64,255,000,000

This serves to paint an interesting picture of our current culture and the economic importance of American brands globally. We should remember, however, that any such number is, despite its specificity, only a numerically expressed opinion.

Persistently irrational behaviour

The financial values attributed to brands are indicative of the economic value they create for companies. This value is caused by creating persistent irrational behaviours, or seemingly irrational behaviours, in customers.

Alongside the balance sheet, strong brands have been shown over time to create price elasticity of demand. That is to say, the company can charge a premium for the product without dramatically affecting market share. People will pay more money for the same product. Additionally, stronger brands with large market share, also, with very few exceptions, have more buyers within a certain time period, and more loyalty as measured through repeat purchase. This is known as the law of *double jeopardy*, which seems to be an empirical fact in marketing (or as close to one as we have).

Initially observing popularity of Hollywood actors and media products, researcher Andrew Ehrenberg demonstrated that the double jeopardy law generalized for brand purchases and applies across categories as diverse as aviation fuel and laundry detergent.[36] Indeed, laundry detergent Tide's brand is so potent at maintaining a price premium that is has come to be used as a currency (see case study below).

CASE STUDY

In 2012, investigators were trying to understand why supermarkets in the United States were being robbed every month of Tide detergent – and *only* Tide detergent. As with every investigation, they 'followed the money' only to find that Tide *was the money*. Bottles of Tide had become an ad hoc street currency, with 150-ounce bottles being exchanged for $5 or $10 worth of drugs, earning it the nickname 'Liquid Gold'.

As *New York* magazine pointed out: 'this unlikely black market would not have formed if they weren't so good at pushing their product'.[37] It turns out that despite being considered a 'low interest category', people have very strong feelings about their detergents. Tide came in the top three brands that consumers were least likely to give up during tough times. This bond has allowed the producer, Procter

& Gamble, to charge 50 per cent more than the average detergent and yet it still outsells its nearest competitor, which is also produced by P&G, by more than two to one.

So, what is it about Tide that means more people will pay 50 per cent more for a functionally parity product from the same manufacturer?

The investigating sergeant puts it well: 'I'm a No. 1 Tide fan', he says. 'I don't know if it's all psychological, but you can tell the difference.'[38]

The dark side of brands

Brands and their purveyors have long longed for authenticity, or at least to be perceived as authentic.

Bizarrely, when discussing authenticity, and the desire that real people have for relationships with real things, what usually happens is that advertising people end up equating authenticity with grass roots, real life, non-commercial stuff. This is odd because, by its very nature, a commercial brand cannot be that, which means any attempts to be so are not authentic.

Being authentic as a brand, or person, is really simple. Stand for something, establish a consistent mode of behaviour and then express it through everything you do, communications and commerce. It's when you say one thing and do another that you stop being authentic. To thine own self be true. (When a brand tries to fake a grass-roots movement, which has been done many times, it is called *astroturfing*.)

One way for brands to feel more authentic in how they act is to embrace their dark side. I first encountered this idea from Adam Ferrier, a trained psychologist, strategist and author of *The Advertising Effect* (2014). He pointed out that in the 1980s brands were all yang: superficial, aspirational, glossy – think any Pepsi commercial, think huge logos. In the 1990s brands developed a more authentic voice, reflecting our actual values not our aspirations, trying to stand for something beyond themselves: think Dove, Innocent, Body Shop, Big Brother.

Following on after this manufactured authenticity then, brands can look to embrace their shadows. Shadows are qualities deemed socially unacceptable and thus are usually hidden, by brands and by people. But if brands could tap into them, they would allow consumers to express and normalize the negative feelings they all have, and thus build much stronger relationships.

To create stronger, robust, believable brands, we can turn to the dark side, exploring a broader range of emotions. One aspect of this can be seen in the recent emergence of 'sadvertising'.[39] Pushing against the hyper-positivity and levity modes that had once again come to dominate advertising, a raft of advertising appeared that tried to squeeze some tears from the eyes of the supposedly cynical consumer. Humour is a powerful advertising tool – it captures attention through disrupted expectations, which also triggers memory formation, and people like to laugh, so it drives favourability. But humour is perceived as being a shallow emotion, while tragedy is the 'highest form of art'.[40]

P&G created its first-ever television spot for itself – rather than one of its brands – with its tearjerker announcement of its Olympics partnerships, claiming to be the 'sponsor of moms', in an ad called 'Best Job'.[41] Dove's 'Real Beauty Sketches'[42] – showing women describing themselves to police sketch artists to demonstrate how critical they are of their own appearances – brought tears to eyes all over the world, becoming the second most viewed ad ever on YouTube.

However, it is not in the *either/or* that the power of myth lies. As Lévi-Strauss pointed out, and as was later discussed by Adam Morgan in his book *Eating the Big Fish* (1999), strong brands solve contradictions. This is because they operate in the realm of myth, and the cultural function of myth is to resolve contradictions. The most obvious example that many myths try to resolve is the fact that we are alive but one day will be dead.

This thinking was enshrined in the thinking of Crispin Porter + Bogusky – 'agency of the decade' (the noughties), as a 'cultural tension' to be solved by the brand, or the idea, and subsequently spread throughout the industry.

Apple makes computers *human*. Persil makes dirt *good*. Dove makes beauty universal. Nike makes everybody an athlete. Google makes infinity manageable. Kodak makes moments last forever. Honda makes (the power of) dreams physical. Starbucks makes luxury affordable. Virgin is a giant that takes on the giants for the little guy. Coca-Cola makes ubiquity unique. At the heart of many cultural tensions is the dichotomy of social beings: how to be unique as part of a group.

Life is full of contradictions. Brands, like myths, provide a meta-narrative that helps people to find meaning and resolve these contradictions imaginatively, since they cannot be solved rationally. Which is why we have Dark M&Ms. Probably.

Brandgrams

In Daniel Schacter's book, *Searching for Memory* (1996), he puts forward a curious description of memory. According to Schacter, memories are encoded in the brain as engrams – essentially a neuron-firing pattern – that captures certain elements from the experience. Certain kinds of encoding are more likely to promote higher recall – specifically, elaborative encoding that allows you to integrate new information with what you already know.

This explains why successful advertising often leverages existing referent systems by making our brain process information and link it to things already in our heads, which means there is a much better chance that we will remember it. Something you know is linked to something you don't.

So brand experiences will build *brandgrams* in our heads.

So far so good, this all feels pretty logical. But then Schacter veers off. What he suggests is that the act of remembering is not really a recollection – it is a new experience: 'The cue combines with the engram to yield... an experience that differs from either of its constituents.'[43]

So the cue, the piece of communication, combines with the brandgram to create a new experience that 'differs from either of its constituents'. People are not simply experiencing the communication but the gestalt of the communication and their pre-existing brandgram.

Now that's what I call consumer-created content.

PART TWO
Attention deficit disorders

Uncovering hidden persuaders
Why all market research is wrong

No one really knows why humans do what they do.
DAVID REYNOLDS

If someone asked me... which half of my advertising is wasted I would probably say 90% is wasted but I don't know which 90%. **NIALL FITZGERALD, CHAIRMAN OF UNILEVER**[1]

The drivers of human behaviour are complex, multivariate and largely subconscious, which suggests that research conducted using claimed data is not enough to gauge underlying causes or the effects of advertising. Advertising functions in different ways depending on context, which suggests that a unified theory of 'how advertising works' will be forever beyond reach. That doesn't mean that 90 per cent of advertising is wasted, simply misunderstood.

Let's lay this oft discussed issue to rest, shall we?

I have long espoused the view that *all market research is wrong*. The idea of researching a market makes sense to anyone who is about to invest money into engaging with one, using products, services or communications. However, the basic idea underlying most market research is epistemologically specious. That is to say, it seems to make sense but, under examination, it does not.

In essence, the foundation of market research is that, by asking lots of people questions, or asking a smaller group of people more in-depth questions, we can gather dependable insight into why they buy what they buy, and whether or not they will buy something in the future, perhaps after having seen some advertising.

I don't believe this is true. For two very simple reasons:

- *We don't know why we do what we do.* We make these (and most) decisions at a subconscious level, which means, by definition, that the operations of the process are inaccessible to our conscious minds.

   That does not mean that people won't answer, though. They will happily answer, erroneously, in a way that seems to make sense, as their minds create fictions to explain their own behaviour to themselves and the interviewer.

- *The gulf between claimed attitudes (and intentions) and actual behaviour is vast.* Asking people if they intend to buy something is analogous to asking them if they intend to go to the gym – the results may not correspond well with future behaviour. Focus groups are particularly fraught: they create artificial data as a response to artificial situations and social dynamics.

Why do we do what we do? It's a staggering question that humanity has ruminated on since it began ruminating. The fact that we don't have an answer yet, the existence of a substantial psychoanalytic industry and the success of cults such as Scientology that claim to have answers all indicate that we don't really understand why we behave the way we do.

A desire to understand what drives purchase decisions, and thus find out which advertising is wasteful, led to simplified models of behaviour such as AIDA,[2] and the purchase funnel (see below). Working out what motivates people to make economic decisions is an area that lies somewhere between psychology and economics. What is confusing is that these two areas of enquiry have very different models.

Psychologists of various flavours look to understand human cognition and behaviour from many angles. Freud developed the therapeutic approach known as psychoanalysis to uncover the 'unconscious patterns of life' that drive behaviour.[3] Psychoanalysis fell from favour in the psychological community, but in recent years the impact of the unconscious has once again come to the fore, with books such as *Subliminal* (2012) by Leonard Mlodinow claiming that our unconscious mind *rules* our behaviour.

The study of interactions between conscious and unconscious elements of the mind in influencing behaviour have been dubbed the 'new unconscious', in order to distinguish this from the old unconscious of repression that Freud was so fond of. This is not to be reductive. Clearly what we think must have some impact on what we do – and what we buy. At least that is what we assume, because that is how we experience it. But even that certainty is being challenged.

Harvard psychologist Daniel Wegner, in his paper, 'The Mind's Best Trick: How we Experience Conscious Will',[4] puts forward the counter-intuitive notion that what we experience as volition is an *epiphenomenon* – a secondary result of the decision being made, not the cause of it. That is to say, our conscious attention may not even be necessary to direct our own behaviour.

This is really hard to get your head round, but various experiments suggest that our experience of consciously making decisions can happen after the decision has been made elsewhere in the brain, which turns logical models like AIDA upside down and inside out.

If it all seems terribly complicated and confusing, that's because it is. The brain is the most complex thing we currently know of. We know very little about how it creates the emergent property known as consciousness. Combine that with the fact that it is interacting with stimuli, some of which are the equally complex minds of others, in the ever-changing soup of culture and commerce, and you have the most complex multivariate system in the known universe. And it is this system that market research seeks to decode in order to increase the efficacy of marketing. It's little wonder that it's a bit tough.

Classical economics, on the other hand, *is* reductive. It is founded on the concept of 'homo economicus' – or rational man – that acts to obtain the highest possible well-being given all available information. This simplified decision model created the division between psychology and economics. It was this fissure that led psychologist Daniel Kahneman to develop what is known as 'behavioural economics'.

The traditional purchase funnel is an *explanatory fiction*: these fictions are constructs that purport to explain phenomena. They tend to obfuscate areas of ignorance by 'filling in the gaps' between antecedent and correlated subsequent events. This is a particular problem in behavioural science due to the creation of agents that are equivalent to the self, and thus provide no true understanding, simply another layer. The simplification of the purchase funnel, in its linearity, doesn't correspond to real behaviour and doesn't explain drivers of behaviour.

First, people don't act this way – numerous other factors interplay with an assessment of needs and gain. Second, in the modern world of brand decisions, products mostly have functional parity. Any advance made by one is quickly followed by its competitor, so tangible benefits, and the consideration thereof, give way to intangible ones in the era of brands.

Behavioural economics emerged as a challenge to the assumption of rationality, attempting to incorporate some of the learning from psychology, and thus it helps to further highlight some of the drivers of purchase behaviour. Additional motivating factors matter such as other people's behaviour – people do many things by observing others and copying; also incorporated was the importance of habit in decision making.[5] Mark Earls suggests that 'the most important characteristic of mankind is that of a herd animal',[6] and studies have shown that consumers 'adopt patterns of routinised purchase behaviour'.[7] So, what we are seeing is that there are numerous factors that impact consumer behaviour that operate without our direct attention.

Despite the addition of these considerations, 'ordinary people remain tantalisingly unique and unpredictable'.[8] So it behoves us to consider how research may help unpick the influences on purchase decisions. The majority of market research is based on claimed data: asking people what they think about brand communication, whether they remember it and why they do what they do. This is obviously flawed, since people don't know why they do what they do. When asked, they will generate an answer that minimizes cognitive dissonance, or the gap between how they think they should act and how they do.

Thus people will tend to give rational reasons for the purchase decisions they make in order to 'justify [their] behaviour to [themselves]'.[9] The spotlight of attention on past behaviour casts an inaccurate shadow on the wall of the cave. Further, 'the gulf between the information we publicly proclaim and the information we know to be true is often vast'.[10] This is what the Market Research Society suggested was responsible for pollsters' failure to predict the 1992 UK general election results accurately – the *Shy Tory Factor*: people lying to researchers because they were embarrassed about voting for the Conservative Party.

As lots of experimentally demonstrated behavioural economics shows us, attitudes are not a good indicator of behaviour, and framing, context and subliminal associations are hugely important drivers of choice, but we are unaware of this. Awareness of subliminal effects negates their impact. This is worth repeating for clarity. If we have our attention directed to subliminal stimuli, they no longer have the same effect. Attention actually *prevents* their influence.

This is ultimately why asking people if certain media will affect their behaviour is mostly pointless. Forcing people to consider something rationally that operates on an unconscious, emotional level, is always going to give the wrong answer.

In *Consumer.ology* (2010) Philip Graves examines these issues in persuasive detail. He points out:

> Ironically, given that the consumer research that feeds it fails to take it into account, it could be argued that most marketing leverages the unconscious mind, and indeed it must do in order to be effective. In many consumer experiences it is either impractical or impossible to compare the array of products on offer. To operate efficiently, consumers rely on their unconscious mind to make decisions.[11]

There are lots of examples in the book that demonstrate the impact of unconsciously perceived variables in controlled research tests. A 1990 study done using Nike shoes by *The Smell and Taste Foundation* placed two identical pairs of shoes in two identical rooms, with one difference: one was scented with pleasant floral tones, the other unscented. According to the study, a staggering 84 per cent of people exposed to the shoes in the scented room expressed higher levels of preference for the shoes, and were willing to pay $10 more for them, on average.[12] It is unlikely that people believed that the fragrance made them like the shoes more, but it seems that it did.

Despite rigorous testing of new consumer products in research, 80 per cent of them fail. Conversely, with the product Red Bull researchers concluded that 'no other product had ever performed so poorly in consumer testing; the look, taste, and mouth-feel were regarded as "disgusting" and the idea that it "stimulates mind and body" didn't persuade anyone the taste was worth tolerating'.[13] And yet by 2006 the company had sold more than 3 billion cans.

Market research is an $11 billion industry in the United States but all the data it generates should be understood as wrong. Now, that doesn't mean we should get rid of all of it. Just because it's not good at making predictions, that doesn't mean it's not useful. It just needs to be used appropriately.

Asking people questions is simply one way in which we attempt to create a model of the infinite complexities of human behaviour. And, as George Box said: 'all models are wrong, but some are useful'.

Asking people what they think is not a pointless mode of enquiry, it is simply not substantive or predictive on its own. Claimed data is useful for exploring attitudes, for understanding what people think they think. Since they are unobservable, the only way to explore them is via careful questioning. The Implicit Association Test developed at Harvard demonstrates one way of exploring these and also serves to remind us that our conscious attitudes may not be consonant with our unconscious attitudes.[14] It uses questions about beliefs, and then times your responses to certain associations to help uncover the difference between what you think you think, and the associations your brain implicitly makes – hence the name. This is because we now know that the brain more rapidly processes associations between things it has already linked than other associations.

However, attitudes can only be used to 'predict behavioural intentions, rather than actual behaviour'.[15] Further, 'individual tendencies do not necessarily extrapolate to group behaviour'.[16] So how are we to uncover the hidden persuaders of behaviour?

I believe research should be thought of as triangulation: any one reading is unlikely to illuminate but a combination may do so.

Interviews should be supported by research that does not rely on individuals to tell researchers anything directly and that looks at the context in which brand decisions are made.

Ethnography is one way to 'zero in on... customers' unarticulated desires'.[17] As an observational mode it is not subject to the flaws inherent in claimed data and it is 'founded in the idea that a system's properties cannot necessarily be accurately understood independently of each other',[18] thus acknowledging the importance of context. However, ethnography incorporates an additional limiting factor: the observer effect, which suggests that 'people change their behaviour when it is observed'.[19]

Advertising is traditionally pre-tested to gauge its efficacy. Traditionally this testing takes the form of exposure to the advertising copy and then interviewing and surveying. Like all claimed data, this approach is hindered. Thus this mode of research also requires a supplement, ideally in the form of physiological response testing such as functional magnetic resonance imaging (fMRI) and galvanic skin response in order to gauge the emotive impact of the communication, which may be beyond conscious cognition.

Millward Brown's LINK testing stipulates the founding requirement for all pre-testing, which is also applicable to all research into the influence of advertising: the 'chosen approach should be based on a sound model of how advertising works'.[20]

Graves suggests that if you want to understand behaviour, you must:

- *Observe actual behaviour*: because claimed attitudes and intentions don't correlate.

- *Observe it surreptitiously*: for as soon as someone knows they are being researched, their responses are suspect.

- *Observe it in context*: because context is such a vital driver of behaviour.

- *Observe with loss factored in*: saying you will buy a product in a focus group doesn't force you to make a choice that loss aversion will flag; there is no opportunity cost to *saying* you will do something.

No rational messaging

Decades of research have demonstrated that rational messaging seems to have little impact when changing behaviour, and that emotional response – regardless of how it is generated – is what does.

Robert Heath, of the University of Bath, found that:

> advertisements with high levels of emotional content enhanced how people felt about brands, even when there was no real message. However, advertisements which were low on emotional content had no effect on how favourable the public were towards brands, even if the ad was high in news and information. So, in advertising, it's not what you say, but the way that you say it, that gets results.[21]

Paul Feldwick, building on this in a seminal paper, '50 Years with the Wrong Model', goes further:

> Somehow 30 seconds of entertaining nonsense leads to a situation where people not only choose this brand but will pay 35% more for it. But somehow it seems we're not very comfortable with this. Because we all like to believe deep down that we really choose our tea on rational product-based grounds.[22]

Looking for substantiation of this point, we turn to a meta-analysis – an analysis of many other analyses – of the Institute of Practitioners in Advertising (IPA) databank. The IPA is the trade body in the UK and hosts the papers of the IPA Effectiveness Awards, one of the few advertising award shows based on business efficacy, rather than creativity. The meta-analysis concluded that: 'The most effective advertisements of all are those with *little or no rational content*'[23] (emphasis added).

Here is a meta-cognitive error at work – a persistent error in thinking about how we think. Our brains like to think they are rational, and so they explain our actions to ourselves with rational stories. Thus, we created the 'advertising as message transmission' model, and so we continue to lean on product propositions as the core element of creative work.

But that's not really how we think and, more recently, Nobel prize-winner Daniel Kahneman's magnum opus, *Thinking, Fast and Slow* (2011), presents the emerging science behind this. His model divides consciousness into two systems: 1 and 2. System 1 works automatically, rapidly, using heuristics to guide decisions and thinking. System 2 is the more linear thinking that we use to work out maths problems, logical and slower. His work presents a direct challenge to the messaging model of advertising, since, as he pointed out during a talk in London: 'You must recognise that most of the time you are not talking to System 2. You're talking to System 1. System 1 runs the show. That's the one you want to move.'[24]

Advertising is mostly conceived, due to the persistent meta-cognitive error of rationality, as trying to persuade System 2 – but that system rarely makes purchase decisions. You can't persuade System 1, that's not the way it learns or decides. It's automatic and associative. This is also what causes some of the problems with market research's ability to be predictive – the conditions of research activate System 2 thinking, when purchase decisions will usually run through System 1.

Research as marketing

That which was private, can now be easily made public. It used to be that you did research and then it informed marketing. Now research can be marketing, and marketing can be research.

One new way of understanding what groups of people think they think, instead of bespoke surveys or groups, is to undertake research on Facebook (or any digital platform), amongst people who have already selected your brand or interest. This research, as a side effect of its public nature, could also function as marketing, for example as teasing the launch of a new product to your existing fans. Research undertaken in front of 1 million Facebook fans is marketing.

As a general rule, it seems most appropriate to phase communication this way. Anyone who has elected to receive communication directly from a brand surely deserves to be told of any new announcements coming from a brand before it hits broadcast channels. And before *they* are told anything, every single person who works at the company, who is, in effect, a brand ambassador, should have been communicated to. This inside-out approach to communication is increasingly important when every single employee has a social media foghorn.

Social media have a tendency to make private things public and thus cut across legacy silos of organizations, which suggests that perhaps we need to stop thinking about these things as separate and consider the whole field – research, marketing, customer relationship management (CRM), customer service – as elements of back-and-forth brand conversations.

In some ways, brands don't really have any choice. Customers understand that the same entity is operating regardless of where we encounter them, and they have come to expect some kind of structural cohesion and understanding among those elements. Today, the single disgruntled customer can have disproportionate impact because of the scale and public nature of social media, in a way that was impossible a few years ago. Equally, brands and businesses have an opportunity to address negative issues in a public way that could earn them additional credibility instead of being detrimental to their business.

Customer service is marketing

CASE STUDY

When musician Dave Carroll's Taylor guitar was damaged in transit on United Airlines, he attempted to deal with the matter using standard customer service channels. He says that after nine months of fruitless negotiations, he decided to write a song about it. The song 'United Breaks Guitars'[25] has had more than 12 million views on YouTube, with more than 150,000 in the first day it was posted, which prompted United to get in touch and try to make amends. Finally, Rob Bradford, United's managing director of customer solutions, telephoned Carroll to apologize and to ask if the carrier could use the video internally for training. 'United mentioned it hoped to learn from the incident, and to change its customer service policy as a result of the incident.'[26]

So what is the moral here? What did United 'learn from the incident'?

In some ways, it is odd that companies have customer service representatives, since the whole function of a company is to serve customers. Normally, *customer service* is actually problem resolution. Carroll claims that he was endlessly passed around the system, each member claiming to be unable to take responsibility or make amends, until he finally took to YouTube. As Ken Wheaton, editor of *Advertising Age*, points out: 'You should be addressing consumer complaints the right way during the very first round... It's always nice when these stories have a happy ending. But it shouldn't take public humiliation for a company to do right by its customers.'[27]

Perhaps the key problem in customer service is representatives who won't give you a name or way to contact them directly; they bounce you around the system, leave you on hold, and finally drop the call when you become too irritating and there's *nothing they can do*.

Individuals want an easy life – humans are like electricity, following the path of least resistance. Working in a call centre for the minimum wage doesn't tend to make people especially invested in the brand they represent, so they palm off customers, get rid of them, drop the call. In fact, many call centres offer bonuses on call volume, so it is actually going to cost an operator money to keep talking about this problem that they haven't been empowered to solve.

One of the things that social media are driving is the breakdown of the corporate firewall. Tony Hsieh, CEO of Zappos, once tweeted:

> If you don't trust your employees to tweet freely, it's an employee or leadership issue, not an employee Twitter policy issue.

Whilst this is a nice thought, it's a lot easier to be open like this if you are small and act that way from the start. Big corporations have structures, legal departments and other inertia that makes this hard, but there is a huge opportunity here.

Until recently, these complaints were locked into an individual's sphere of influence, which was limited until social media gave everyone a voice. However, social media are, usually, overheard, because they operate in public by default.

So there are two directions in which this can go:

1 Companies can keep acting like one person doesn't make a difference and see how much time, effort and creativity that one person will deploy to get his or her frustration out into the world, as Dave Carroll did – and see how receptive the world is to such messaging.

2 Decide that customer service is the most important thing a company does. The only route to long-term profit is *making customers happy* – so do it in public, reach out to people, don't put the onus on the individual to battle through the firewall or the 800 number. Constantly monitor the social web for people who are unsatisfied with the product or service you sell and, as long as the complaint is justified, do what you need to do to *make them happy*.

Then, customer service becomes marketing, because solving real people's problems in public is a compelling testament to your approach, and every person you make happy will sing your praises across the web. In a connected age, a happy customer becomes an advertisement, especially on Facebook, as Mark Zuckerberg has pointed out:

> The whole premise of the site is that everything is more valuable when you have context about what your friends are doing. That's true for ads as well. An advertiser can produce the best creative ad in the world, but knowing your friends really love drinking Coke is the best endorsement for Coke you can possibly get.[28]

What brand tastes like

Why *do* people love drinking Coca-Cola?

In *Predictably Irrational: The hidden forces that shape our decisions* (2008) Dan Ariely illustrates a truth that we find hard to accept, which is that we are not rational beings. We make decisions that are seemingly irrational – in the same way, again and again – because of how our brains are hardwired: anchors and priming, emotions and context all interact to change how we choose. All these impact behaviour while operating below the attention threshold.

One of the things Ariely highlights is the power of expectation to alter experience. He describes a replication of the famous Coca-Cola/Pepsi taste tests, done with the subjects in an fMRI to record how their brain is processing the experience of tasting the drinks.

In the original blind taste tests, Pepsi usually wins, but when the brands are revealed, people prefer 'the Real Thing'. According to the experiment detailed in Ariely's book, this is because the experience of consuming branded sugar water is different from drinking sugar water alone: the Coca-Cola brand activates different associations in the memory and emotional parts of the brain, which contribute to the consumption experience, which means that when you drink a Coca-Cola a part of what you are tasting is the brand.

For Christmas 2011, Coca-Cola created some limited edition polar-bear cans for Classic that were predominately white, rather than red. People mistook it for Diet Coke because it was white – and Coca-Cola pulled the cans, citing consumer confusion. But perhaps it was more than simply confusion. Consumers 'felt that regular Coke tasted different in the white cans'.[29]

Taste, like every sensory experience, happens in the mind, so it is more complex than just chemicals – it happens at the intersection of lots of things, including, of course, the chemicals and your tongue, but also including less obvious things such as expectation (being told you will love this), concepts of value (this wine is very expensive), where you are (anchoring/priming) and memories associated with it.

Coca-Cola officials denied changing the taste, but changing the can dramatically can also *change the taste*. Changing some of the key cues around the product can distort the brand effect and change how people experience the taste.

Physical persuasion (nod your head)

Start nodding your head while you read. Go on, it will be fun. Keep doing it until you forget.

In *The Tipping Point* (2000) Malcolm Gladwell highlights a piece of research that students were told was for a company making headphones. The recruits were given headsets and asked to perform specific motions while listening to music and a piece of editorial concerning a rise in tuition fees. One-third of the recruits were told to nod, one-third to shake their heads, and one-third to remain still as a control group.

Afterwards they were asked some questions in an attempt to gauge how persuasive the editorial had been on them. The control group were unmoved by the editorial. Those who shook their heads from side to side while listening, ostensibly to test headphones, strongly disagreed with the proposed increase. Those who were told to nod up and down found the editorial very persuasive. They wanted tuition fees to rise. The simple act of nodding their heads while listening was sufficient to cause them to agree with a policy that would take money out of their own pockets.

The authors of the study concluded that:

> Television advertisements would be most effective if the visual display created repetitive vertical movements of the television viewers' heads (eg *bouncing ball*).[30] (emphasis added)

This is partly to do with the way our eyes track motion. We tend to follow curved motion along its own pathway, moving our heads slightly. For reasons that remain unknown, our attention is more directed by curved motion than rectilinear motion.[31]

If one bouncing ball is persuasive, how persuasive are 250,000? (Are you still nodding?)

In 2006, Sony, with their advertising agency Fallon, launched a small creative renaissance in their communication with the spot 'Balls'.[32] The lead creative behind it was Juan Cabral, who tore a hole in the London advertising scene in the mid-noughties, only to vanish back to Argentina to make 'beautiful films', as he liked to say.

Fallon had picked up the global account, and was looking to make work that resonated globally. Laurence Green, then planning partner of Fallon, and one of the smartest minds in the UK advertising scene, relates how the idea came about:

> Juan Cabral (for it was he) suggested 'we bounce thousands of balls down a hill and film it'. We asked him to turn this mere bagatelle of an idea into a proper script. Two weeks later, he came back with: 'We bounce thousands of balls down a hill and film it.' (He was right, of course.) And so Sony's, Fallon's and maybe even advertising's fortunes shifted.[33]

Watching 250,000 balls bounce up and down, gently, in slow motion, to an acoustic guitar cover of the song 'Heartbeats' by José González was persuasive enough to make Bravia the world's bestselling TV, to push Sony back into profit and give it back its bounce.[34] It became one of the most loved and awarded advertisements of all time.

Now, I'm not saying that Juan Cabral had the persuasive power of nodding in mind when he had the idea (he may have had the David Letterman stunt from 1996 in mind where David threw 50,000 coloured rubber balls down a hill in San Francisco), but I am saying that nodding may well have helped to persuade people to like the ad and to like Sony, when it came time to buy a new television, or to give some advertising awards, despite the fact that they were not aware of this.

(Do you agree? Are you still nodding?)

Advertising works in mysterious ways
Modern theories of communication

I Watched an Ad

i watched an ad
it made me smile
i was 10% happier for a while

i watched an ad
it was a bore
far too easy to ignore

i watched an ad
it sold with sex
indistinguishable from the next

i watched an ad
i like the tune
must remember to download it soon

i watched an ad
eliciting guilt
and mourned over the milk it spilt

i watched an ad
'call this number!'
an order i tend to cast asunder

i watched an ad
and like the rest
i denied it its request

there is no ad
that's worked on me
all brands bark up the wrong tree **LAITH YAKOB**

How do advertisements work? On the surface, advertising seems very simple. Use mass media to create awareness for the products you wish to sell, usually focusing on some specific benefit, expressed in a creative way to catch the attention and convince large numbers of people to buy it, increasing revenue by more than the cost of the campaign.

Yet, the more we learn about how humans think, decide and behave, the more we realize that those things are derived substantially from processes hidden from our view. Attention is slippery. Advertising campaigns rarely pay for themselves in the short term,[1] but their effect can last for decades. The notion of a universal model for understanding how advertising works is misguided. The difference between the drivers of the purchase of baked beans and a car are vast, because the difference between the nature of these decisions is vast.

It is remarkable that the two currently favoured models of how advertising works, which in turn provide templates for how companies behave, are diametrically opposed. On the one hand we have the engagement model. This suggests that brands that develop deeper relationships with consumers, that invite them into a dialogue and deliver additional content and experiences, that stand for something the consumer can ally themselves to, will be most successful. This is particularly true in today's fragmented, attention-starved world. Engagement is about *earning* attention.

On the other hand, Robert Heath has convincingly demonstrated that 'low attention processing' is a powerful driver of behaviour. His position echoes, perhaps consciously, a maxim by Marshall McLuhan: 'Any ad consciously attended to is comical. Ads are not meant for conscious consumption. They are intended as subliminal pills for the subconscious in order to exercise an hypnotic spell.' Heath suggests that overt attempts to engage higher cognition are challenged. Those preferences we pick up subconsciously are much more powerful. He argues that the 'perceptual and conceptual elements we learn *implicitly* are stored as associations with the brand' and that 'implicit memory is more durable that explicit memory'.[2] Since implicit learning is automatic, it is functioning every time we experience an ad, whether or not we pay attention. Therefore, brands that follow an engagement strategy are likely to be *less* successful than those that exist at the peripheries of consciousness at high frequency. Heath, following McLuhan, is suggesting that advertising should not interrupt attention at all, in order to better slip into the mind unexamined. How are we to reconcile these two models?

Heath's analysis is not based on a new idea – it echoes Vance Packard's *The Hidden Persuaders* (1957) – and is supported by substantial data. It feels intuitive since people remember jingles from their childhood but struggle to remember other specifics with clarity. That said, it also makes intuitive sense that brands that deliver value and engage in ongoing relationships with consumers will establish favourability, a metric that historically was shown to be a corollary of purchase intent. (This is why intuition alone is never enough.) Who wants to buy products from companies they don't like?

The answer is not either/or: we don't need to reconcile the two differences. There are different models that work in different ways, and are appropriate for different objectives and contexts. A number of different models of advertising are valid, and communication planning requires an understanding of the differences between them. This is not a new idea either (as we'll see later, there are no 'new' ideas): 'No single theory or group of theories can explain it all, because advertisements work in such different ways. There is no point in looking for an overall theory.'[3]

Some brands will benefit from developing engaging communication, some from adhering to a low-involvement strategy. The question becomes when to use which and this depends on, as it inevitably must, the consumer and their needs. Media strategist Ben Kunz has suggested that engagement strategies work better for consumers who have varied needs, whereas broadcast communication is more relevant for mass audiences who have similar needs. He adds in personalization strategies, which are outbound messages pushed to smaller numbers, and research-led approaches, where many people need to research the product, usually due to higher costs (see Figure 3.1).

The important thing to remember is that each task requires the right approach or mix of approaches. Not every problem can be solved with the same solution set, which is a challenge for many agencies, who too often assume their primary product is the optimal solution.

FIGURE 3.1   The information ecosystem

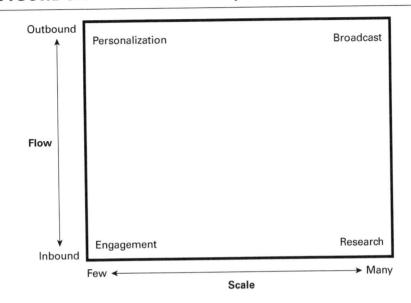

SOURCE: Ben Kunz/Media Associates. Used with permission

The moment of truth

When does it all pay off?

A brand, from the point of view of a person, may be considered like a memory: every brand experience builds to develop an engram – a specific and evolving pattern – in a person's mind. This *brandgram* is triggered by encountering additional brand cues and these cues combine with the brandgram to create a new experience. This final experience at point of purchase, when the cue of the product itself combines with the brandgram, will ultimately drive a purchase decision. Procter & Gamble, packaged goods giant – and the world's largest advertiser – calls this the 'first moment of truth': the three to seven seconds when you first see a product on the shelf in the supermarket. The *Wall Street Journal* suggested that 'despite spending billions on traditional advertising, the consumer-products giant thinks this instant is one of its most important marketing opportunities'[4] – but this misunderstands the point. Rather, it is at this moment that the totality of all previous brand interactions either pay off or don't. So the nature of the experience is what needs to be considered – what does the consumer require when making this purchase decision?

Consumers need different brands to do different things. The vast majority of purchases do not adhere to a purchase funnel at all – they are made impulsively. Shopping at the supermarket, when confronted by innumerable varieties of baked beans, we choose a brand 'because it doesn't matter that much and it makes stuff easy'.[5] To avoid pointless cognition every time we go shopping we use brands as heuristics to shortcut decisions. Since there is, or there is perceived to be, functional parity among the primary competitors, we need to have only a very slight preference for a brand to aid the decision.

Other purchases have different contextual needs that brands help to fulfil. High involvement purchases, such as consumer electronics and cars, have a longer purchase cycle, although there are indications that it is decreasing thanks to better access to information. There are always a combination of rational and emotional needs that brands satisfy. Engaging communication that helps to build stronger brand affiliations, a more developed sense of the brand, can help to provide the consumer reassurance, both pre and post purchase.

The needs of consumers and the drivers of their behaviour are variable. By looking at some of the veiled aspects of attention and cognition we can begin to understand better people and brands, and how they interact.

Lubricants of reason

It's not emotion or reason, but always both.

Fooled by Randomness (2001) by Nassim Taleb was hailed as one of the 'smartest books of all time'.[6] It is an exploration of the huge, underappreciated role of randomness in life.

Taleb looks to understand the stochastic limits of epistemology. His core thesis is that we think we know how things work, because our brains like cause and effect so we apply a deterministic model to observations. This leads us to make mistakes and leaves us open to being 'blown up' (trader lingo for losing beyond what you believed possible) by very rare events of huge magnitude.

Taleb dismisses classical economics as pointless due to its reliance on the increasingly hollow rational man construct. Unfortunately, we are intellectually wed to binary oppositions, so once we realized that emotions had a role in decision making, an opposition was established between rational and emotional persuasion in communication. Maybe we make some decisions emotionally and some rationally?

Thanks to people such as Phineas Gage, who have had accidents that damaged their amygdalae – the almond-shaped groups of brain nuclei involved in emotional reactions – we know this simply isn't true. When people lose access to their emotions, they are no longer *capable of making decisions*. We like to think of ourselves as rational beings, but without the heuristics of emotion to help us, we would never be able to decide anything.

So it is not that there are emotional and rational sides pulling us in different directions but that emotions are the 'lubricants of reason' – we can't think without them. This is expressed nicely in a recent theory of decision making known as the somatic marker hypothesis:

> Real-life decision making usually involves assessment, by cognitive and emotional processes, of the incentive value of the various actions available in particular situations. However, often situations require decisions between many complex and conflicting alternatives, with a high degree of uncertainty and ambiguity. In such situations, cognitive processes may become overloaded and be unable to provide an informed option.
>
> In these cases (and others), somatic markers can aid the decision process. In the environment, reinforcing stimuli induce an associated physiological affective state. These types of associations are stored as somatic markers.[7]

This suggests that the role of communication could be simply establishing or reinforcing the somatic markers in association with brands, so that when consumers encounter the decision of which toothpaste to buy, the markers kick in and lubricate the decision, preventing paralysis and panic attack.

Brands take away the need to choose by covertly biasing cognition, thus making our lives easier.

The paradox of choice

We have too many choices to pay attention to all of them.

In the United States (even compared to the UK) there are many more options to choose from, especially on the supermarket shelf, which groan under a bewildering array of alternatives in every product category. More options = more brands = more ads.

Choice is equated to freedom, and freedom is a necessary condition to ensure the inalienable right to pursue your own happiness. More options mean more freedom, which means more happiness. Or so they say.

Except it doesn't work that way.

Barry Schwartz points out in *The Paradox of Choice* (2004) that having too many options tends to make you unhappy, which is why he argues that hyper-capitalist economies, which sanctify individual autonomy and thus force decisions at every possible opportunity, tend to be less happier overall.

This insight is compelling because it feels right and yet wrong – the idea of freedom underlies the cultural foundation of Western society. Counter-intuitively, people know that they love choice but find that they hate making decisions.

People will do almost anything to avoid making difficult decisions – ones where there is no clear, obviously better option. An experiment undertaken by researchers at Columbia and Stanford universities highlights the conflicted drivers of consumer behaviour. In the study, shoppers at an 'upscale grocery store' encounter a tasting booth that displayed either 6 or 24 different flavours of jam to try. The 24-flavour jam table attracts more people ('amongst all those options there must be the right jam for me') but, having been attracted, they were forced to make a difficult decision ('there are too many to choose from and I just don't care this much about jam'), which ultimately led to the 24-flavour jam display selling one-tenth as many jars as the 6-flavour display.[8]

Dramatically increasing the number of options decreases the propensity to purchase. Decisions with lots of options cause anxiety, paralysis, proleptic regret and a bunch of other negative responses. They increase the effort invested in the decision and ultimately can diminish the enjoyment you get from anything you do choose. *The Paradox of Choice* explores these negative psychological effects in detail and suggests a strategy to avoid them, which is essentially to lower your expectations and seek to make a *good enough*, rather than the *best*, decision ('satisfice don't maximize').

But we've developed another way to help deal with this problem, at least at the supermarket: brands. In advertising we spend a lot of time thinking about what brands are and how they work – what they are for. Brands are good for companies because they increase frequency of purchase, allow you to charge a price premium, drive loyalty, are a defensible competitive advantage and contribute significantly to the intangible asset value of a company, as we have seen.

But what is the function for consumers? What value do they offer to individuals that creates the persistently irrational behaviour that drives shareholder value, that means people pay more money for essentially the same thing?

The function of brands has evolved as the nature of the economy has evolved. In early capitalist economies, industrialization created large corporations that distribute across massive areas. Brands functioned, and still do, as *trustmarks*, ensuring that you get what you expect when buying from manufacturers.

But in hyper-capitalist economies, since we achieve functional product parity in most categories, every minor purchase decision becomes difficult. There is no clear, obviously better option, which makes a supermarket an uncomfortable prospect. According to a Research International report, 46 per cent of shoppers spend more than three minutes in front of the shelf, picking up an average of three products, when actively making a decision. The number of brands in all categories available on supermarket shelves has multiplied in the last 20 years. According to the Food Marketing Institute, there are nearly 44,000 items crying out for your attention in the average supermarket.[9] Customers are trying to be responsible, informed consumers, but multiply three minutes by the total number of grocery items in a weekly shopping trip for a family of five, and you have a significant time and cognitive burden. Additionally, as Schwartz points out, the more options, the greater the opportunity cost associated with any single purchase (ie every other option that solves the same need).

Brands come to the rescue. They function like heuristics – they take away the need to make decisions, take away the pressure of pretending to ourselves that we are rational economic agents, prevent us from breaking down every time we want some jam. Eventually, this can lead to habitual shopping behaviour, with customers 'sleep-walking' through the supermarket, buying the same things again and again.

CASE STUDY

It was this insight – that customers buy the same things again and again – that drove a successful advertising campaign for UK grocery retailer Sainsbury's. Facing long-term declining sales in 2004, AMV BBDO wanted to wake up consumers from 'sleep shopping' and they used advertising asset Jamie Oliver – now a food brand in his own right – to encourage customers to 'Try Something New Today'. This was more than simply an exhortation, as it was supported with recipe cards in-store, training for 150,000 staff, and point-of-sale signage, all of which provided suggestions for something new to try. According to the IPA Effective Award it won, it generated $2.5 billion in extra revenue over six years.

Even if you don't default to the market leading brand in the category (although you are obviously more likely to) you can anchor the category to it, allowing you to make a decision in relation to it. We are very bad at making absolute decisions, and tend to make them relative to the set of options available.

So, as emotions are the lubricants of reason, brands are the lubricants of commerce.

Blindness blindness and meta-cognitive errors

Our attention dictates what we see, but we find it extremely hard to believe that this is true.

Illusions often highlight features of how our attention system works. The 'invisible gorilla' test effectively demonstrates *inattentional blindness*, where we don't see something even though we are looking directly at it. Designed by neuroscientists Daniel Simons and Christopher Chabris, it consists of a video and a set of instructions. You are asked to watch the video and count the number of passes made by one of the teams – the video is ostensibly of two teams playing basketball.[10] When the video ends, you ask the viewer if they noticed anything unusual. Most people do not. Then you play the video clip again and pause it in the middle, whereupon the viewer is startled to see that a man, dressed as a gorilla, has walked into frame, stopped to beat his chest and then walked out again, and yet somehow you missed it. Your attention was focused on counting passes, and so you simply don't see the gorilla, because your brain is actively suppressing distractors from your task. It is important to note that it's not because your eyes don't fall on the gorilla – eye-tracking studies demonstrate that people do not notice the gorilla *despite looking directly at it.*

It is a phenomenon of mind, not eye. To quote two colleagues of the neuroscientists: 'To truly see, you must pay attention.'[11] This presents compelling challenges to the media unit of currency, known as *impressions*, as we will see in the next chapter – they can only ever offer an 'opportunity to see', which by definition is also an 'opportunity to miss', if people are not paying attention.

Change blindness is a related perceptual phenomenon where we don't see something because our attention is elsewhere. The canonical experiment on change blindness involves a door. Someone stops a student on campus and asks for directions. Then, while directions are being given, workmen carry a door between the student and the person seeking directions – at which point, the person is replaced with someone else. Amazingly, those giving directions almost never notice.

This is how perception works: making sense of visual data is an act of *filtering out unimportant information.* In this context, our attention is focused on directions. The reason *we think* it's amazing that people don't notice, which is also the reason that this experiment works, is because of a meta-cognitive error called 'change blindness blindness'.[12]

We rarely notice significant changes in the visual field when our perception is disrupted by things like interruptions, saccades or their filmic equivalent, tracking shots. But we tend to think we will. Even when we are shown that we don't. This is because it deviates from what we believe about how we see.

We believe that our eyes beam reality directly into our brains, because that's how we perceive perceiving... but they don't. Only the very centre of our visual field sees things in detail – this is called foveal vision, after the centre of the retina. Only when we focus on something do we 'see' it in detail, and if we aren't paying attention, we don't even notice it then.

When we shift our attention rapidly, it triggers other perceptual glitches, such as the stopped clock illusion. If you flick your eyes over at an analogue clock, people often experience the illusion that the second hand freezes for a second. The theory suggests that this is a function of how we perceive – our brains are trying to smooth out reality. When you shift your attention, most obviously by moving your gaze rapidly, a break in the information is created and needs to be 'covered up'. So your brain fills in the gap with what follows the shift – hence the second hand stutters. A glitch in the matrix of your mind. Our attention changes the world we see around us.

To further confuse things, both novelty *and* familiarity can capture attention. As we will see, things that disrupt our expectations create preferential looking: *new* and *improved* is horrendously overused on goods packaging because manufacturers know it hacks your attention system (as do typographic disruptions **LIKE THIS**). This is why consumer packaged-goods manufacturers constantly introduce new variants, formulas and designs. This 'product news' captures attention. This is also why the core creative belief espoused by many advertising agencies is 'disruption' (TBWA) or to be a black sheep, to zag when others zig (Bartle Bogle Hegarty). Alex Chaldecott, founding partner of a great 1990s UK agency, Howell Henry Chaldecott Lury, said that the 'HHCL experience taught [him] you must challenge convention constantly, otherwise you won't produce anything distinctive'.[13] It seems everyone is challenging the status quo, because they want to capture attention through novelty, but it does make you wonder what is left to be the status quo.

Familiarity creates preference because it lessens the cognitive resources needed to process the stimuli. This is known as the *mere exposure effect* – people tend to develop a preference for things merely because they are familiar with them. When a stimulus feels more fluent, the way people process decisions relating to that stimulus tend to be more intuitive and less thought through. These mechanisms clearly underlie how some advertising works.

The complexity and varying modalities of how we allocate attention, and how that impacts decisions, is why advertising works in mysterious ways. Let's look at a few.

Disrupted expectations

Disrupted expectations seem to lie at the heart of many emotional responses. It's what lies at the heart of most jokes:

> An incongruity of register is comic on account of its recognised deviation from the expected norm. This stress on expectations makes it feasible to reduce the joke, for example, to the product of a set of formal criteria (a build up of expectations followed by a disruptive punchline) without paying any heed to what the joke is about.[14]

Deviation is also what triggers attention. Preferential looking, the 'tendency of infants and children to peer longer at something that is new, surprising or different',[15] indicates that infants pay more attention to things they perceive as unexpected.

A fundamental aspect of cognition is the necessity of forming expectations, based on direct or indirect experience, for how things are in the world. Research based on this idea suggests that there are all kinds of cognitive and affective events triggered by expectancy violation, including heightened memory activity, which makes sense as your brain is rebuilding part of its model of the world.

This is why comedic advertising works so well, since jokes capture attention and elicit emotion at the same time. It is also why magic works:

> Magic tricks work because humans have a hardwired process of attention and awareness that is hackable – a good magician uses your mind's own intrinsic properties against you in a form of mental jujitsu.[16]

Magicians manipulate our attention to shift focus away from where the trick may be exposed. This is what we call misdirection. Advertising can also be understood as the capturing and manipulation of attention, for that which is within the spotlight is highlighted, and surrounding elements are suppressed, as suggested by its etymological root.

Mind the curiosity gap

Curiosity is an emotional response that motivates exploration. A lot of animals have this instinct (including cats), which suggests it is a hardwired cognitive mechanism. As such, it is a potent communication tool: if you can make someone curious, they become naturally inclined to do something, which translates to shifting behaviour, moving them towards you or your brand.

Curiosity is stimulated by making people aware of manageable gaps in their knowledge. How does this work? First, you have to show people enough of something to get them involved, but leave enough gaps that people feel the need to fill in themselves. If you give people all the answers, there's nothing for them to do.

The New York agency Campfire, who were involved in early branded Alternate reality games (ARGs) such as Audi's Art of the Heist[17] (where a new car was seemingly stolen from a showroom, leading to a multilayered online and offline scavenger hunt), and The Blair Witch Project, says the key to great communication that is shared is 'managing the curiosity gap'.[18] Scatter information across channels, and communities will form to collect and share it – these are the underlying principles of *transmedia* properties, which are stories that play out across a number of non-linear media channels.

CASE STUDY

This approach was embraced by JJ Abrams to promote the movie *Cloverfield* – a 'monster movie for the YouTube generation'.[19] The trailer seemingly found footage, screened without warning being announced.[20] Simply by not really explaining what the film is about, or indeed what it is called, the movie triggered a flurry of media and consumer attention six months before it was released.

The trailer became mainstream news, hailed as something that 'transforms marketing'.[21] The film had an estimated budget of US $25 million. The unusual marketing helped to drive the film to make $40 million in its opening weekend. It went on to make more than $170 million.

Pandemic, or viral is a thing that happens, not a thing that is

Clients will sometimes ask for 'viral videos', to which one should reply 'viral is a thing that happens, not a thing that is'.

If people pass on your communication, it is viral, or at least has viral potential. If they don't, it is not. It is a measure of success. Having a viral strategy is akin to having an Oscar strategy. You can create better chances, but you cannot guarantee it. (At least, that is what one hopes about the Oscars.)

If a video is not being shared, the problem is usually that it is an ad that contains nothing people consider worth showing to their friends. People share content for social reasons – we use content to communicate. Viral is a behaviour of the audience not a property of the content, which is why the metaphor does not work very well. The brand is piggybacking something else that is being passed on – usually entertaining content or social currency.

This brings me to the launch of directory enquiry service 118-118 and the vests, the Campaign of the Year in 2003 in the UK.[22] It was created with a number of elements we hoped would be adopted by the audience. But the bit that was most electively shared, where consumers became the communication vector, was the vests worn by the two characters in the commercials. People stole the vests (that were hung out for them to steal) and they wore them – and still do. More than 10 years later, they continue to appear at festivals all over England. (I've even seen one on Bondi Beach in Sydney. That makes it a pandemic.)

But, for the sake of clarity in our metaphors, let's get rid of the word viral entirely. My brother, Laith Yakob, who is an epidemiologist, has pointed out that the 'viral' metaphor is flawed – ideas do not propagate through populations like diseases. The metaphor is seductive and difficult to get rid of. There are agencies that specialize in 'viral ideas' – including one in the Ukraine with the unfortunate name Ebola Communications. The metaphor reaffirms a structure of control. It implies that all you need to do is to create something that is 'viral' enough and it self-propagates. This is untrue.

What we mean when something goes 'viral' is that lots of people choose to share it, for their own reasons. It is not simply a new way to broadcast our messages through populations. It suggests we push, when in fact they pull.

As Duncan Watts, researcher at Microsoft, has pointed out, the structure of the network is as important, and perhaps more so, in predicting the spread of content than the nature of the content – the same thing can succeed or fail depending on network structure. By saying something *is viral*, we focus on the content itself and not on the needs of the people that we are asking to spread ideas. As media theorist Douglas Rushkoff says: 'people don't engage with each other to engage viruses; people exchange viruses as an excuse to engage with each other'. Like so much communication, it has a social function, both phatic and generous. It operates within a gift economy, where value is generated in transference. Further, if you let people mess with your content, it is more likely to be shared because they like to share things they are a part of. Instead of attempting to create 'virals', we should be trying to understand what people would like to spread – and why.

CASE STUDY

Any fool can make soap – it takes a clever man to sell it

Soap has ever been the archetypal advertised product. In fact, one of the founding fathers of modern advertising, Thomas J. Barratt, was a brash young marketer who took a soap, A&F Pears, and made it, undeniably, a brand.

By 1789 Andrew Pears had devised his transparent soap, but until the middle of the 19th century it had been very modestly advertised. In 1865, when the firm's annual bill for advertising was £80, Thomas J. Barratt, a young man of 24, became a partner in the firm, and ushered in a vigorous new regime. This is detailed in *The Shocking History of Advertising* (1952) by ES Turner.

Barratt is on record as saying: 'Any fool can make soap. It takes a clever man to sell it.' When he took over control of Pears he raised his expenditure on advertising from £80 to £100,000 (making him, I can only imagine, the world's most loved client) in order to establish the brand as the default for the category, intuitively leveraging a number of concepts that we have looked at such as low attention processing, copied behaviours and more.

Barratt's policy was summed up with perfect simplicity in one of his own advertisements: 'How do you spell soap? – Why P-E-A-R-S, of course.' 'Pears' and 'soap' had to be linked so deeply and ineluctably in the public mind that it would be impossible to think of one without the other.

It is wrong to say that no one reads advertisements; they are not there to be read, but to be absorbed, just as a capsule is not meant to be tasted, but to be swallowed.

The visual attack did not satisfy Barratt, however. He decided he must have a catchphrase that would make the whole country say 'Pears Soap'. His staff were invited to nominate the commonest phrases in daily use. Inevitably, someone suggested 'Good Morning':

> *The result was the notorious 'Good Morning! Have you used Pears Soap?', which scourged two continents. There were many who never forgave Thomas Barratt for debasing this traditional, friendly greeting. The sensitive shrank from saying 'Good Morning', knowing that it would only spark off the exasperating counter-phrase in the mind of the person addressed.*[23]

The attention market

People in advertising have traditionally taken a dim view of borrowed interest. The thinking was that using 20 seconds to tell a joke and the remaining 10 seconds to sell was not a great idea. There are assumptions underlying this summary judgement:

Borrowed interest just means there's no real value in the product or service you offer, or at least the [advertising] agency people couldn't find it, or were more concerned with a 'creative' portfolio that might impress other ad people.[24]

This thinking is flawed. It assumes that the function of advertising is to express a differentiating truth about the product or service, which makes you want to buy it – that advertising is solely salespersonship, but it is not, at least not any more.

No unique promises about what a product does can be maintained for any duration. The perceived veracity of such claims on people have begun to suffer under their endless repetition. According to research firm Nielsen's Global Trust in Advertising Survey, people claim that their trust in traditional advertising is in long-term decline: 'Nearly half of consumers around the world say they trust ads on TV (47%), in magazines (47%) and in newspapers (46%), but those numbers dropped by 24%, 20% and 25% respectively, in a relatively short period of time – between 2009 and 2011.'[25]

'Borrowed' interest is a sound strategy for attracting attention. PG Tips borrowed from the chimps, Cadbury's from the drumming gorilla, the burger from the King, the insurance broker GEICO from the lizard or the caveman and so on. Leveraging existing cultural artefacts – such as the expression Good Morning – and appending your products, you borrow interest to attract attention. In fact, you could argue that it is *creating* interest in something that is not itself interesting, by connecting something relatively boring (most products, in most categories, are by now exceedingly familiar) to something else. You can ladder up your product benefit to a higher order value proposition, but all your competitors could too. It is impossible to 'own' any such positioning as a brand:

- Clients tend to think their products are fascinating because, if you spend your life thinking about something, it takes on great significance in your mind.

- Agencies tend to think that what they do is interesting, but one of the first things you learn at an agency (or should learn) is that marketing clients only spend a fraction of their day thinking about advertising, although it is perhaps the most visible element of their roles.

- Calling people 'consumers' tricks you into thinking they spend their whole lives buying stuff, or thinking about buying stuff. But they really are not that interested.

This is why things are so different now. We cannot really buy enough attention any more: media are too fragmented, people have become too good at not paying us any. Instead, we are increasingly expected to earn it, to get into the 'consumer's' media streams.

Previously, the implicit value – free content in exchange for watching ads – enabled the balanced exchange between brands and people. This model is best encapsulated by Homer Simpson: 'Quiet, the commercial is on… if we don't watch these, it's like we're stealing TV!'[26]

But that relationship has begun to break down in an on-demand world. *Wired* magazine suggested that we are now in an 'attention economy'.[27] The internet is a live, global attention market, dynamically allocating attention to those things that earn it.

Understanding how attention is being allocated across the market is the next big frontier of analytics: Google, innumerable social media tracking companies, behavioural targeting and retargeting intermediaries, all attempt to track, understand and ultimately predict the allocation of attention. This data has value – it is the commercial engine behind Google, Facebook and most of the web. This is live, aggregate data, not survey-tracked brand awareness scores.

It has become a cliche of the digital age: if you are not paying for an online service, then you are the product being sold. Part of the shift we need to embrace is wrestling more of that value back for the individual – imagine if you could trade attention, receiving value in return.

Back during the gold rush of the first dot-com boom, a company called All Advantage tried to redress the attention issue and balance the value exchange by paying people to watch ads. It also compensated members for promoting the site, which made it grow rapidly.

The company died – paying people to watch ads has been demonstrated not to be the right way to think about value. It didn't work years later for mobile startup Blyk, which offered free calls and texts in exchange for watching advertisements on your phone.

Thinking about value that way feels analogous to paying someone to be your friend – it is still buying attention, not earning it. People don't like to believe they can be 'bought'.

Moore's Law is now the driving force of change in media. Moore's Law is, in fact, more a trend of hardware computing history than a law per se. Gordon Moore, the founder of Intel, described in a 1965 paper how the amount of transistors we can squeeze on to an integrated circuit board doubles roughly every two years, as the cost halves. This in turn means that computers get faster and cheaper, and memory gets cheaper as well:

- The price of a gigabyte of memory in 1981: $300,000.

- The price of a gigabyte of memory in 2010: $0.10.[28]

- In 2014, Google offered cloud storage of a gigabyte of memory for $0.026.

This tendency to exponentiate is the biggest driver of change in your world and it is really, really weird. Nothing else changes like this. Cars don't get twice as fast and half as expensive every two years. Neither do refrigerators. In fact, nothing does except computers, specifically transistors. And now so does media, because ever since media became digital, and therefore a function of memory, the amount of available media bandwidth is also a function of Moore's Law.

With the internet, we have, essentially, infinite media space. And, practically, infinite amounts of content, thanks to that media we call social. We are in a stage of transition, where human interpersonal networks are going to supplement or even to some degree substitute commercial broadcast networks. Facebook is turning itself into a media browser, where content being shared is the primary way we see anything – over half of all content sharing online is done on Facebook.[29]

Media products act like *solidarity goods*. If no one sees it, it's not worth anything. The more it spreads, the more eyeballs it accrues, the more it is worth. Thanks to filtering algorithms like Facebook's, which decides what appears in your Facebook feed, if content is not shared it may not get seen at all. As media professor Henry Jenkins has written: 'If it doesn't spread, it's dead.' The algorithms are constantly revised, but one constant has been that they tend to add weight to content that has been shared electively by your friends.

The importance of being awesome

Did you know that the word 'awesome' used to mean roughly the same thing as terrible? Both were used interchangeably to describe the presence of God – something that inspired awe and terror. It is in this sense that awesomeness is important for brands, media, ideas and people – because of a fundamental shift in the nature of the mediascape.

Everyone is making content and culture all the time, which presents new kinds of challenges – how do you get any attention in an infinite space? Awesomeness is (at least part of) the answer. It turns out that emotions spread, and that awesome content is the most spreadable.

Studies done by the *New York Times* show that the most shared articles on their site are ones that *inspire awe*.[30] Specifically, things that are epic in scope and require 'mental accommodation by forcing the reader to view the world in a different way'.

'They're seeking emotional communion', said Dr Berger, professor of marketing at Wharton, University of Pennsylvania: 'Emotion in general leads to transmission, and awe is quite a strong emotion... If I've just read this story that changes the way I understand the world and myself, I want to talk to others about what it means. I want to proselytize and share the feeling of awe.'[31]

So if you want people to see and share your content – make it *awesome*.

Is all advertising spam?

Communication planning in an on-demand world

Attention is the rarest and purest form of generosity.

SIMONE WEIL

If we extend current trends in media fragmentation, channel-centric thinking by the advertising industry could lead to both the end of advertising as it is currently conceived and the emergence of a new model of communication. The media-industrial complex has historically delineated itself by *channel*. Press is one channel, with associated planners and buyers and creatives who work best in it. Television is another. Somehow 'digital' became another but it is not – rather it functionally subsumes other channels – all media will become 'digital'.

Ultimately media channels will become redundant constructs and new designations will have to be created, based on an understanding of people's relationship with content and how they consume it. While this signals the decline of media planning (because dictating when and where content will be encountered becomes impossible for much of an on-demand world), it also indicates that strategic communications planning will become crucial to reach and develop solutions for consumers.

The rapid proliferation of media channels is well documented and shows no sign of abating. 'We now live in a society where almost anything may be explored for its potential as a medium'[1] – and in an attempt to find uncluttered space to communicate, brands have moved further and further beyond traditional channels.

Digital technology has changed the nature of what we understand as a medium. The internet is inherently bidirectional – anyone who receives can also broadcast. It works in a fundamentally different way to the media we knew before. It is not simply a new channel to push messages down but an ever-growing suite of channels that have infinite space and no fixed form. Anything that can be mediated can be rendered in bits.

Traditional media planning is a product of the pre-digital age. Its principal aims, 'to faithfully (without distortion) transmit messages [and] to reach specified target audiences... with most effect, least waste [and] least cost',[2] indicate the assumptions upon which the practice is based. Namely, that channels are not dynamic contributors to meaning and that, ultimately, the efficient transmission of messages to receptive consumers is the goal.

The underlying assumption that this relies on is the *impression – one set of eyeballs seeing a brand message once.* This is a conceit implying that an impression delivered via any channel is equal. Thus, gross ratings points (GRPs) may be totalled up across channels for a campaign. They are 'directly calculated by summing the ratings of individual ads in a campaign'.[3] They measure both *reach* and *frequency*, which is to say the percentage of the target audience reached and the average number of times they saw an advertisement. If an 'ad campaign results in 50% of the target seeing the advertising 3 times on average, then the campaign's size was 150 GRPs'.[4]

The idea that all impressions are equal is patently false, as it pays no attention to how people actually parse media. If media planning is simply about delivering efficiencies, it will become a function that can be replicated by software. Indeed, programmatic media buying has already taken the industry by storm in the United States, where software dynamically bids and allocates digital creative inventory in fractions of a second, through a bewildering array of networks and other 'ad-tech' intermediaries.

Constructs such as 'demand-side platforms' – trading desks for digital advertising inventory that manage multiple exchanges – allow media agencies to arbitrage value out of inventory by appending data to display ads, based on the previous behaviour of the viewer, thereby increasing relevance and accuracy.

Unfortunately, because so much technology is involved, no one really has any idea what is going on with the billions of fragments of attention being bought and sold. As digital media spend approaches $50 billion in the United States alone, marketers chase attention as it darts around the web.

The Interactive Advertising Bureau, the trade body for digital advertising that created the standardized units that allowed digital media to be used across the web, admits that: 'about 36% of all Web traffic is considered fake, the product of computers hijacked by viruses and programmed to visit sites'.[5] That means more than $15 billion is being spent by software to buy the simulation of attention from other pieces of software! Research by Comscore suggests that 31 per cent of online ads are unseen because they cannot be seen – they are placed in areas of the site that users cannot see.[6]

The total number of digital advertisements served (sent from a server to a webpage being viewed) was 5.3 trillion in 2013 in the United States alone. That is about 14.5 billion digital ads every day.[7]

This is a staggering amount of exhortations. We are dealing with numbers that are increasingly abstract and removed from any understanding of how these pieces of communication might be impacting people and each other. And all this is only possible due to the earlier sleight of hand that made impressions into a currency in the first place.

It was this insight into the implausibility of the impression's nominal fungibility that led to the use of qualitative research as an input into communications planning, which helped planners to understand 'the quality of the media environment within which a brand appears'.[8] However, we need to move beyond the idea of *confronting* consumers.

The military vocabulary of media planning – targets, campaigns, executions – exposes an underlying assumption: brands are at war with consumers. The proliferation of media outside the traditional has often been akin to ambushing consumers in unexpected places (suitably known as guerrilla marketing).[9] Indeed, Russell Davies, the former head of strategy and insight at advertising agency Wieden+Kennedy (W&K), has co-opted a term for this: urban spam.[10] I believe we can extend the definition further. I believe we can describe all advertising as spam.

Whilst considering direct mail, it became clear to me that the key differentiator of whether I would open and read it was whether or not I had requested it. If I had opted in, then the communication was welcome. However, commercial messaging sent to me that I did not request, is junk mail or spam, which is irritating and increasingly filtered out by e-mail clients. This is at the heart of Seth Godin's concept of permission marketing.

Integrated marketing communications (IMC) took a step beyond the traditional model of media planning. It advises the 'strategic co-ordination of all marketing messages and the alignment of all methods of communicating'.[11] Whilst this goal of semiotic and strategic unity is worthwhile, it is no longer adequate as it does not address the problems associated with using ever-increasing amounts of interruption to capture finite amounts of attention.

As Seth Godin comments: 'As the marketplace for advertising gets increasingly more cluttered, it becomes increasingly difficult to interrupt the consumer.'[12] As Godin goes on to point out, the response from brands has been to increase levels of spend on interruption, an escalating battle. Broadcast interruption marketing is 'unsolicited, unwanted, irrelevant... commercial advertising in mass quantities'[13] – which, online, is a definition of spam.

As all channels become digital, some consumers will extend the definition of spam to them, and can use technology to block it out. Ad-blocking software usage online is growing. A report by monitoring service PageFair suggests about 1 in 5 of all web users now use ad-blocking software, which costs sites large sums of money in unmonetized viewers.[14] As the battle continues, 'the pool of people who will accept ads is smaller and smaller and those ads get more aggressive and intrusive to target them, and then those people get annoyed and seek out ad blockers', says Neil O'Connor, CEO of PageFair. 'It's a vicious cycle.'

This is already beginning to be apparent on television, with the advent of the digital video recorder (DVR). According to Forrester research, 92 per cent of ads are skipped by DVR users.[15] Increasingly, consumers have control over how they consume the content they want. Even if advertising is not actively filtered out, it could be argued that it is cognitively filtered by those who live in the glare of the endless war against clutter. This passage from Neal Stephenson's novel *The Diamond Age* (1995), which foreshadows a future-shocked Times Square, already seems very familiar:

> Unremitting exposure to this kind of thing produced mediatron burnout among the target audience. Instead of turning them off and giving people a break for once, the proprietors had joined in an arms race of sorts, trying to find the magic image that would make people ignore all the other adverts and fix raptly on theirs. The obvious step of making their mediatrons bigger than the others had been taken about as far as it could go... Once all the mediatrons were a hundred feet high, the only competitive strategy that hadn't already been pushed to the redline was technical tricks: painfully bright flashes, jump-cuts, and simulated 3-D phantoms that made bluff charges towards specific viewers that didn't seem to be paying enough attention.[16]

We must question this model of advertising during periods of accelerated change. This led Steve Heyer, the chief operating officer (COO) of Coca-Cola at the time, to maintain that: 'in today's marketing and media environment only the naive and foolish confuse presence with impact'. Tackling the impression illusion he asked: 'do we need reach and frequency – no. We need idea driven connection with our targets.'[17]

The age of interruption marketing is slowly drawing to a close. Digitally empowered consumers will question value unless the value is explicit or the trade is laid bare, giving them the options to pay for the content or view advertising. The escalation of brand interruption on the populace has brought about this situation, so that consumers now actively reject commercial messaging, or at least believe they do.

Using the internet changes the way people think about all media in relation to it. According to one study, the more spam and pop-up ads that consumers encounter, the angrier they are about all forms of advertising – online banner ads, event sponsorships, even radio and television advertising.[18]

The discrete nature of channels themselves is no longer an entirely useful way to understand them. Marketers have traditionally thought of each medium as distinct – this is why media agencies are often structured into buying departments by medium, especially as buying attention in each 'channel' grows increasingly complex. With the advent of digital channels, content can flow freely from one to the other: audio-visual content, for example, can be consumed in innumerable ways: on televisions, computer screens or personal media players. Audio can be broadcast, streamed or downloaded as a podcast. Tablets allow for the fluid transfer of print.

The boundaries between many of the standard channels are dissolving as we shift to a media consumption model based on content and screens. IBM suggests that the new world will be characterized by 'platform-agnostic content and the fluid mobility of media experiences'.[19] Increasingly, this content is pulled by the consumer, not pushed on to them as in the broadcast model. Whilst there will always remain some ways to invade the consumer's awareness, for example using formats such as billboards that cannot be 'switched off', thinking in these terms is ultimately flawed, as it maintains the idea of brands locked in a battle of attrition with consumers. Developments such as the Philips television patent that disables the ability to fast-forward through the ads, and the battle over similar functionality in Dish TV's Hopper DVR product, are indicative of this kind of thinking and will generate resentment and antipathy towards brands, which is diametrically opposed to the desired outcome.

It also fails to take into account the fact that digital platforms have given rise to a new kind of media consumer who rarely gives their full attention to any one channel. Rather they give 'continuous partial attention'[20] to a number of different streams. This has major ramifications for media agencies built around specific media silos, and further erodes the concept of the impression, which is a 'one dimensional metric'.[21] TV or print buyers become unable to suitably assess the value of multimedia packages. Frustrated media owners who have broken out of this single-mode mindset (how many TV channels lack a website?) are increasingly going directly to clients with these packages.

Thus, as AdAge warned, 'media agencies [are] in danger of becoming obstacles, not enablers', which is also why they are championing the algorithmic approaches at one end and developing branded content specialties at the other.[22] This also presents interesting new opportunities. The connected generation are consuming more media than ever, to the point where 'there's almost a discomfort with not being stimulated – a kind of "I can't stand the silence".'[23] They are 'media meshing': surveying a number of channels simultaneously and navigating between them – 'to complement information, perspective, and emotional fulfillment'.[24] Brands must respond to these dramatic changes in consumption.

If brands can no longer force their messaging on empowered consumers, if attention can no longer be bought in large enough quantities, how are they to influence purchase behaviour, drive loyalty and develop and maintain a price premium? The problem with traditional models is that they focus on the transmission of the message to consumers (Figure 4.1). Despite protestations of putting consumers at the heart of this process, it ultimately only considers the needs of the brand in this exchange. Consumer profiling looks to understand how the various touch points via which consumers may interact with the brand can be best utilized to influence the said consumer.

This bias probably stems from the fact that only 'the transmission of... brand stimuli is within the control of the marketing company – their reception is not'.[25] From the consumer's point of view, there is an unbalanced value exchange occurring. The individual consuming the marketing message is giving up value in the form of time and cognition: attention (Figure 4.2).

This may seem trivial but it is of great value. Value is derived from relative scarcity and 'attention is the scarcest resource of the 21st century', and consequently of significant value – something people

FIGURE 4.1   The traditional model of advertising

FIGURE 4.2 The value exchange of traditional advertising

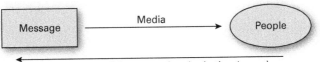

are increasingly aware of. Research by PR giant Edelman confirms that people see 'relationships with brands as one sided [&] limited in value'.[26]

Previously the value exchange came entirely from footing or supplementing the cost of the content being consumed, but increasingly the array of content options, ability to screen out interruption and the disaggregation of content from its sponsors by technology brings this into question for people. Therefore, communication in the connected age needs to deliver value as well as messaging. This balances out the value exchange, making the communicative interaction equitable. Importantly, the value needs to be an expression of brand behaviour, delivering the brand's values via 'transitive action'.[27] Let's call this value-added communication. Since it delivers value, consumers will not avoid it and it will engender empathy for the brand, not resentment – it is not spam. Interruption advertising will still function, no doubt, but its use is broadened to introduce prospects and customers to other elements and actions.

Brands often claim to desire relationships with their customers or fans. Relationships are mutually reinforcing – providing value to both parties, and dynamic – responding to the needs of each other over time via two-way interaction (Figure 4.3).

FIGURE 4.3 A balanced value of exchange for advertising

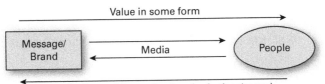

There are innumerable ways to deliver value and many brands have already begun to do this. While delivering utility might be more obvious, a lot of this value is delivered via entertainment and experiences, functions of their emergence as distinct economic and hence added-value offerings.[28]

Early on, Lynx (known as Axe in the United States) championed the movement towards delivering content that their audience will elect to engage with. Gamekillers was a Lynx campaign that launched as a television programme on MTV and was supported with content-driven websites.[29] Half reality show, half guide on attracting the opposite sex, they took the promise of Axe and made it into narrative in a very different way than a traditional advertisement. Content engines like this can create traditional advertising as well. Brands can deliver value through facilitation. Hewlett-Packard (HP) and Red Bull provide platforms for emerging artists.

CASE STUDY

HP's HYPE gallery was an online and offline exhibition for digital art. Once the hottest start-up in the world, HP had become huge and was primarily seen as an enterprise supplier, selling printers and the world's most expensive fluid – printer ink. In a comparison done in 2012, HP 60 cartridges of colour ink cost US $5,654 per litre, whereas Chanel N°5 cost $3,180 per litre.[30] HP wanted to appeal to a younger, creative audience, hugely sceptical of the behemoth. So, instead of an advertising campaign trying to convince them otherwise, HP opened the HYPE gallery in London's Brick Lane. Submissions were sought with the only stipulation that the letters H and P had to feature somewhere in each artwork. The artists who uploaded their work would be printed and projected for display in the physical gallery and used as advertising. The online gallery received 4.5 million visits from 145 countries, all for the cost of a conservative, local, advertising campaign. It won two Cannes Gold Lions, was responsible for naming HP Client of the Year, and inspired the birth of the Titanium category at Cannes to highlight innovative work of this nature. You can see the evolution of this idea in HP's 2014 Power Up campaign, a festival in New York that celebrated the intersection of art and creativity across an ever-expanding range of disciplines.

CASE STUDY

Red Bull have created several long-running platforms to foster and celebrate the creativity of others. The Art of Can exhibition has similar aspects to the HYPE gallery. This juried art contest has run every year for a decade and asks people to create works of art using the Red Bull can as the medium. The winning entries are displayed at exhibitions all over the world and online, of course.[31] The Red Bull Music Academy is another long-running programme where budding musicians apply to be tutored by professionals. Alongside the core academy, it hosts workshops, creates content and hosts live events, curates stages at festivals, runs a radio station, an online magazine and a newsletter. This is a kind of open-sourced approach to marketing, where customers become collaborators: their creativity is facilitated and then turned into advertising or content. Brands are able to harness credibility, and perhaps in turn provide fame for work that may have otherwise gone unseen. As my wife Rosie wrote as part of a Content Marketing White Paper: 'Memes created by consumers in a matter of minutes are often more viewed than high-budget commercials. Brands that are able to leverage consumers to create or co-create content on their behalf will hit the sweet spot.'[32]

Intel's Creator's Project is another long-running facilitation platform, developed in association with Vice, the self-consciously alternative media brand. It supports artist projects that use technology in innovative ways and has run since 2010 at events and venues across the world, generating reams of content and making Intel relevant to a generation that no longer worried about the speed of their processor.

Brands need to understand the nature of the content that consumers desire and how they want to access it. In a twist on the old model, brands can offer consumers free or discounted third-party content if they are willing to consume the advertising as well, making the old value equation more obvious and in the hands of the viewer. This model thrives on websites such as Salon and Hulu, where, in some instances, consumers are allowed to select the advertising they would like to watch.

The traditional media model sees media companies using content to build an audience to sell to advertisers. Many of these value-added communications lead to the disintermediation of traditional channels, as brands develop direct relationships with consumers, developing their 'own audience and... content to engage that audience'.[33] The goal for brands is to break down the division between their consumers and themselves, making consumers feel like the owners and producers of the brand, which in reality they always have been.

The question, then, for communication planning going forward, is how to advance a company's commercial and communication goals in a way that delivers value for customers and culture.

An apologia for advertising

The lubrication of capitalism, the creation of emotional value around product consumption, the ability to deploy and navigate commercial signs and let people use them to understand themselves and each other – these are necessary functions in modern culture.

For as long as art and culture has existed, patronage has been required to help support it. Royalty and aristocracy would provide patronage, for a combination of altruistic and image reasons, which allowed art to be created and events for the masses to happen. The nature of this commercial relationship was culturally defined – it was never a simple commercial transaction – and the impact a patron had on the work or event was equally prescribed by convention.

It was, for want of a better word, subtler than simply sticking your name on something. A patron's taste, sophistication and grace – not just their money – were being reflected in how the patronage would manifest.

Today, brands provide patronage, but often forget that it is not just their money that should be evident. In almost every area of culture, brands – rather than royalty – are now the primary means of support. In times of economic uncertainty, in almost every arena of culture it is brand sponsorship that keeps museums open, writers and artists in work, and your favourite website or app in business. As researcher

Danah Boyd says, 'selling out is meaningless' in our modern, commercial world.[34]

Yes it creates exhortations to buy and, yes, the world has lots of problems and too much stuff, at least in the parts of it most laden with brands – but advertising is, like law and banking, something that keeps the wheels going.

If trust in advertising has diminished, trust in law and banking has plummeted since the great financial crisis of 2008. Whilst advertising may be perceived to be manipulative, it works mostly in plain sight and its objectives are obvious. An advertising agency has never been fined billions of dollars for working for Mexican narcoterrorists.

The work we do can increasingly direct how companies behave (as we shall see in Chapter 6), as a function of the changes occurring in the media environment. Tiny, incremental changes, based on changing consumer needs, can have significant impact when they are undertaken by companies the size of Wal-Mart. As the CEO of organic yoghurt brand Stonyfield said, when discussing distribution via the world's biggest retailer: 'if you want to change the way the world operates, you need to marshal your economic power.'[35] When Wal-Mart decided to stop wasting money shipping water across the United States, non-concentrated detergents ceased to exist almost overnight. We have an obligation to advise our clients how best to leverage insight into consumers and culture and communications to make them money.

If you don't want to live in a hyper-capitalist culture, that's great, you are lucky enough to be in a free-enough society (probably, if you are reading this) where you can choose, and every dollar you spend is a vote for the kind of society you want to live in. As the documentary *Food, Inc.* (2008) suggested, companies only ever change their behaviour in response to customer demands. Advertising is ideally placed to help companies to shift and leverage demand – indeed that is, in some part, its *raison d'être*.

There is nothing sadder or more detrimental for the advertising industry than the self-hating, advertising despising, advertising professional. As Cindy Gallup has pointed out, we need to stop communicating the idea 'that advertising is a very bad thing'.[36] We can, and should, strive to make it better. This is the perfect time to do so, as the assumptions of the past 50 years begin to crumble, as the sole god of shareholder value is questioned, we can drive clients and the industry towards earning attention, creating explicit value for companies and their customers.

And that starts with the practitioners.

Martin Boase, one of the founders of storied London advertising agency Boase Massimi Pollitt (BMP), one of the places where account planning – the strategic function of advertising – was created in the early 1970s, put it like this:

> We believe that if you are going to invite yourself into someone's living room you have a duty not to shout at them or bore them or insult their intelligence. On the other hand, if you are a charming guest and you entertain them or amuse them or tell them something interesting, then they may like you a bit better and then they may be more inclined to buy your brand.[37]

More than this even, I like to believe that advertising can be a force for good in the world.

A long time ago, when I got into advertising, I decided that I would prefer it if, and therefore I would work towards the idea that, advertising can be a force for good. I mean, who wants to do something for a living that is considered to be an annoyance or indeed a cultural blight? We, as an industry, have the chance, and I would argue the responsibility, to guide our clients to commercial solutions that might also have a beneficial impact on the world.

Despite loving both Bill Hicks and George Carlin, I don't think that their side is the whole story. (I certainly don't think marketers should all kill themselves, as Hicks suggested.) To quote David Ogilvy: 'Advertising is only evil when it advertises something evil.'[38] Like, say, technology, or any tool, it is what you do with it, and how you do it, and how you think of people, and what kind of person you end up becoming because of it.

Working in advertising can make you cynical, but if you can aspire to look yourself in the mirror and see the kind of person your 8- or 14-year-old self would not hate – not lie or cheat, on clients or your partner(s); treat people and customers and clients and vendors and the world with respect; not attack people or people's work; not be petty and cruel; be open to the opinions of others and be willing to change your mind; not worship money above friendship or honour; not let your heart get hard; stay in love with creativity; spend time working for the good of the industry, especially the young people, as well as for your own career and the agency; treat people as ends in themselves, not simply means; and remain thankful that there are jobs that let you have ideas for a living and wear jeans and T-shirts to work – then advertising is a fine profession and one to be proud of.

The spaces between

The vanishing difference between content, media and advertising

Content and *media* are weird words. They are the antonymic binary stars that our industries circle around, feeding off the energy they pump into culture. They don't exist without each other. Even in the very specific sense in which we use the words in advertising, they are both defined by what they are not:

A medium is a vector for content.
Content is that which is mediated.

Without a medium, there is no content.
Without content, you have no media.

Content is apparently 'king' online but all that means is that people like stuff more than the absence of stuff. Less facetiously, people like ideas. We literally define ourselves (*homo sapiens* literally means wise, or sapient, man) by our ability to have and to hold them. But with *ideas* we hit another semantic issue – there is no other word in philosophy that has quite as many different flavours to it.

I don't mean big ideas, or Platonic ideas. Let's just say stuff in your head. The desired initial result from any communication interaction. I have stuff in my head, I want to put it in yours.

Content/media are a way to do that over time and space, to many heads all at once. Stories are one of the oldest ways of doing that.

Stories survive because they are either entertaining (man's life is nasty, brutish and short, and we tend to like anything that takes our mind off that) or because they are useful – in some cases both.

Originally that usefulness meant 'and lo did Ugggg eat of the purple bush and verily did he die' (I doubt that Australopithecus used a bad Shakespearean register but you get the point), but later that came to be useful in the sense of telling us something about ourselves.

Media making the world

Originally, media was all about recording the world. We wanted to capture what we saw, freeze it in time and space, show other people. Analogue media attempts to re-create the world faithfully, transposing variations in amplitude and frequency to re-create the impact on our senses. It takes a property of a medium and modulates it to transmit information.

In analogue sound recording, fluctuations in air pressure (that we hear as sounds) strike the diaphragm of a microphone, which induces corresponding fluctuations in the current produced by the electromagnetic microphone. That current is therefore an 'analog' of the sound.

Digital media transmit data differently, representing everything as numbers, rendering that into binary: discrete on and off states that computers recompile back into representations of the sensorial world. Eventually, though, it became apparent that the relationship between media and the real world, reality and simulacrum, was not one-way. A medium is a vector, a way to spread thoughts, and these complex things we call ideas are just as good at changing the world as they are at recording it.

This idea called *digital* has encroached upon the marketing industry. The word has come a long way from the Latin for finger, to represent the great change that is rippling through culture thanks to creation and distribution platforms that are available to all.

The first wave of thinking about it was as something discrete: a discipline, a department, something that simply sits alongside the rest of the marketing world. But it's not.

The changes begin to spill off the screen, affecting how we encounter companies and each other, changing expectations, changing how we communicate and even how we think. The industry polarity that starts with analogue and feeds down to digital needs to be entirely reversed, because 'digital' is what is driving the most change in the 'real world'.

Lions and language and geeks

Language is in a state of constant flux, evolving at the edges, occasionally ruptured by changes in culture. It contains fossils and fractures that hint at what has been or will be important.

Within the communication industry (formerly known as advertising), language is rapidly evolving in response to dramatic changes in the context we operate in.

Job titles are an obvious example. Over the last few years new roles have come into existence within advertising agencies – content strategist, social media something, creative technologist, user experience designers, developers, digital ninjas and chief technology strategists – to help us service the growing need to understand and connect to consumers enabled by technology.

The word technology has also changed. It comes from the Greek *tekhnologia*, a systematic treatment of an art. It involves both knowing and doing. Douglas Adams, author and famous technophile, summed up well the recent tension within it (stealing the idea from Danny Hillis, one of the fathers of modern computing):

Technology is a word that describes something that doesn't work yet.

It doesn't refer to normalized technologies, such as writing, or television, but emerging technologies that we don't fully understand yet.

Adams pointed out why this was:

There's a set of rules that anything that was in the world when you were born is normal and natural. Anything invented between when you were 15 and 35 is new and revolutionary and exciting, and you'll probably get a career in it. Anything invented after you're 35 is against the natural order of things.[1]

The 'natural order of things' for the communication industry is perhaps best reflected in the awards that are dispensed, most famously at the Cannes International Advertising Festival, where the 'great' give Lions to the best of the last year, hinting at their hopes for the future.

Increasingly, the big winners have 'technology' at their core. Obama picked up the Grand Prix in the Titanium category in 2008, a category created a few years prior to celebrate breakthrough ideas that point to a new direction, with a presidential campaign that was enabled by social media and crowdsourced participation. In 2013, the Barbarian Group won the inaugural Innovation award with Cinder, a creative coding platform. Getin Noble Bank won an innovation award for creating a debit card with digital display showing your balance. While this is still an advertising festival, these winners are made of Arduino and code as well as art and copy.

The Cyber category is both fossil and prophet (William Gibson's neologism 'cyberspace' has long since fallen out of usage almost everywhere else). The winners here have included the Fiat Eco-Drive,[2] an interactive tool that pulls data from your car and visualizes it to help you drive more efficiently, and Queensland Tourism's 'Best Job in the World',[3] which promoted the islands of the Great Barrier Reef to the world by advertising a job looking after one. Small recruitment ads drove people to a website where they had to submit a video application. The idea generated more than $200 million in global publicity value for Tourism Queensland.[4]

Perhaps most telling is the Film category, which, unlike Radio and Press, no longer conflates content with delivery platform. In 2007 the category was expanded to include 'other screens'. In 2008, for the first time, the Grand Prix was awarded to a film that had never been shown on television. Philips 'Carousel' is an interactive web film that promoted their new cinema-ratio televisions with a single tracking shot through a frozen explosion.[5] At that time this was shocking but it has now become standard. In 2014 a web film called 'Epic Split', featuring Jean-Claude Van Damme doing the splits between two Volvo trucks, won the Grand Prix in both the Film and Cyber categories, as well as gold prizes in the PR, Promo and Activation, Direct, and Integrated, and silver prizes in the Titanium and Media categories.

It stands as a telling example of how digital has destroyed the delineations between channels.

This is 'film' designed for the web, where attention must be earned, where narrative is no longer entirely linear, where technology, whatever that might mean, is helping us to communicate in new ways, with new kinds of craft.

The medium definitely isn't the message, any more

Digitization has done more than erode the delineations between media – it has freed content from its distribution platform.

Think about what we call advertising.

Its traditional form is an historical accident. The nature of what we call advertisements was shaped by the nature and relative scarcity of the transmission vectors available.

We put films on television, and attention is expensive, so we buy it in 30-second chunks, and call those advertisements. The nature of the medium dictated both the form and length, and the time scheduling and consumption grammar dictated the modality of reception, or the mindset and mood you were in when you saw and heard and felt it.

Advertising grew up in a world where media was scarce so we got used to compression and density being key communication skills. A brand or advertising proposition is the densest possible articulation of an idea, the work of a planner who has compressed everything necessary down into the smallest possible space. A tagline opens that meaning back up again, attempts to express as much as possible in the most memorable textual unit.

This is why advertising has long thrived on paronomasia, or punning, because leveraging phonic ambiguities allows you to say two different things at the same time, and when people decode it, it feels satisfying.

However, it is worth keeping in mind that advertising comes from *advetere*, so advertising should perhaps be considered anything that draws attention to a company. We have conflated the expressions with the intention.

Until recently, what we call media were assemblages of a number of different things. 'Television' isn't actually a clearly defined thing as such, it's a sociocultural construct of at least two things: content type and distribution platform. Books, magazines, radio all work the same way. A 'book' is a bunch of words printed on paper, with a certain set of culturally defined ideas that float around it. Until *digitalness*, you couldn't separate the content from the distribution platform – but digital 'content' can be unbundled.

The iPad made me realize that it is not just distribution and content, there is a third piece: the *consumption platform*, the physical thing through which content is consumed, which used to be bundled with the distribution platform, but no longer needs to be.

When you are watching *Orange is the New Black* on Netflix via your Xbox 360, or on a laptop, or screen, or projector, or iPad – are you watching television? If so – why? If not – why not? When you are reading Dave Eggers's *The Circle* on your Kindle (or iPad) – are you reading a book? If so – why? If not – why not? A Kindle is not a book, and yet it is all books, or can be (Amazon launched a subscription service in 2014 that allows you to access the entire Kindle library for US $9.99 per month). The words don't quite fit properly any more because they were bundled constructs that are coming undone.

You have the distribution platform: in pre-digital media these were closed networks: book distributors, magazine distributors, cables, satellites, mobile phone networks. With digital you just need an IP network that you can access anywhere.

Then you have content. Digital content can take any form: text, audio, video, experience, game and so on.

Then you have consumption platforms: screens basically.

Digital media strips content from its distribution platform, rendering everything as ones and zeros, which means, as all media inexorably becomes 'digital' media, all media will be platform agnostic. Content flows across what we previously thought of as channels, and different parts of the system can effect change in other parts, in near as-makes-no-difference to real time.

The content republic

Since the earliest days of what we used to call the information super-highway, a refrain has echoed across industries. A mantra, a koan, an aphorism of our age that guides development and business models, showing us all how to proceed, chanted regularly, religiously, by traditional media companies especially, and increasingly by technology companies:

Content is king!

There are various other contenders for the royal positions on the web. Context is a contender to the throne itself; technology, user interfaces, linking, RSS and XML have all been proposed as queen. Increasingly it would seem that community and connectivity both have valid claims to the crown.

Nicholas Negroponte suggested in his book *Being Digital* (1995) that connections were more important than content when he explained that the 'true value of the network is less about information and more about community'.[6]

The rights and powers of the king are unclear but I think the expression is supposed to mean something like: 'Content is the most important thing on the web and if you have excellent content you will be able to make money, either by selling it or getting some ads around it.' This, of course, isn't true. Nor is it entirely untrue. That's the way the world works with a lot of things.

Previously, we had two basic content monetization models: people pay for it, or advertisers pay for it in return for interrupting the attention it has aggregated. There are some very specific challenges to monetizing content online, which are already tearing apart content industries whose output, digitally, has low storage and bandwidth requirements. Once something exists digitally, it can be copied, perfectly and for free, and redistributed, which introduces a new content model, where no one gets paid – peer to peer transmission.

The prevailing wisdom has been that once consumers get used to something being free online, they don't want to pay for it. iTunes came along and disproved this. It further demonstrated that the way to control content was not reactionary Digital Rights Management, but rather making buying it simple and cheap enough. But iTunes doesn't stop piracy. All the lawyers of the Recording Industry Association of America (RIAA) and Motion Picture Association of America (MPAA) cannot stop piracy, which means that the content ecosystem will incorporate some free content floating around the web.

But there are many ways to skin a content cat.

YouTube has experimented with alternatives to straight advertising. It has announced a test initiative to allow partners such as online university the Khan Academy to charge for downloads. For about $1 you could get a good-quality version of the content, and the copyright holder can set licensing rights as they please. Now, think about what you are buying here – not the content, exactly, more a set of permissions and a convenient way to reuse that content. This is an obviously unmet need, filled by web-based providers such as vixy.net.

It is indicative of thinking outside the old model – if you are not selling the content, what else will people pay for? What makes content more useful?

Bloomberg information services sell information that you can mostly get on Google, for free, 15 minutes or so later. It is not selling the content, per se, it is selling *extra time*. In fact, people could record songs off the radio if they wanted to, but they bought compact discs because that was more convenient. Then MP3s came along, and even though they were relatively poor quality, they were more convenient.

There is going to be room for many different monetization models, based on context and consumer desire. Hulu and Spotify have adopted hybrid *freemium* modes, supported by advertising, which can be lessened or removed by paying subscription fees. Some musicians and game developers have offered pay-what-you-wish downloads.

Asking consumers what they want directly is, as we know, not very enlightening – people don't really know what they want, and are very bad at predicting what they will want. Accenture's Global Broadcast Survey indicates that 49 per cent of consumers would rather pay for content online and avoid advertising. So, some will pay and some won't. As the economics of media remain in flux, we shall continue to experience a Cambrian explosion of business models. When media agitator Chris Morris announced his scheme to crowdsource funding of his film *Four Lions* (2010), a satirical comedy about British jihadists, because Channel 4 declined to do so, it was both launch announcement, publicity stunt, culture hack and funding request.

This hinted at another model: crowdfunding, raising the cost of production in tiny increments from many people, from fans, rather than from a studio. Just as the T-shirt website Threadless produces T-shirts at almost no risk, by gauging interest in advance of production, content producers can reach out into the crowd and see if people will microfinance niche content that would never get made through the mass economics of studios. This hint was picked up by the producers of the much-loved but ultimately cancelled television show *Veronica Mars*, who used the crowdfunding platform to source US $5.7 million for a feature film in 2013.

As the economics of cultural production continue to decentralize, as more 'consumers' become 'producers' of content, content monetization comes under the renewed threat of free. It is economically very difficult to compete with people who don't do things for money. Among the media of the masses, content isn't king, it's a republic.

Of course, there is another sector that produces content, one that is seemingly less concerned about models of content monetization, because it is one: advertising. Brands have been creating the content that pays for the content. However, most advertising is not seen as content – hence the term branded content – because it is assumed to be undesirable. Advertising is about selling products – content is about, well, anything that makes people voluntarily spend time with it.

This suggests that we need to take a long hard look at what we want 'advertising' to be. Either we continue to fund other people's content or we begin to shift the emphasis in the industry. If we spent 80 per cent of budgets on production, rather than the traditional 10 per cent, instead of using it to buy attention, just imagine what kind of content we could create.

That said, of course, creating content that is perceived as valuable and attracts an audience is far from simple, as any media company can tell you.

Cumulative advantage

Duncan Watts, a researcher at Microsoft and the author of *Six Degrees: The science of a connected age* (2003) and *Everything is Obvious Once You Know the Answer* (2011), has demonstrated with 'closed world' experiments that not only is social influence at least as, if not more, important than personal preference when deciding what you like (as counter-intuitive as that might sound), but there is an additional factor that makes it practically impossible to predict what will be a hit:

> The reason is that when people tend to like what other people like, differences in popularity are subject to what is called 'cumulative advantage,' or the 'rich get richer' effect.[7]

This means that if one object happens to be slightly more popular than another at just the right point, it will tend to become more popular still. As a result, even tiny, random fluctuations can blow up, generating potentially enormous long-run differences among even indistinguishable competitors – a phenomenon that is similar in some ways to the famous 'butterfly effect' from chaos theory.

This is why film studies and record companies find it impossible to predict what will be a blockbuster, which led to a venture capital model of cultural production, where studios and labels invest in 10 things on the assumption that nine will break even or lose money but one will make enough to recoup the losses. This is why screenwriter William Goldman famously said of Hollywood: '*Nobody knows anything.*' This portfolio model is also flowing into brand thinking, especially online. The more stuff produced the more hooks, the more chances that something will catch the network's attention.

The writer Cory Doctorow calls this 'thinking like a dandelion':

> Take the dandelion: a single dandelion may produce 2,000 seeds per year, indiscriminately firing them off into the sky at the slightest breeze, without any care for where the seeds are heading and whether they'll get an hospitable reception when they touch down...
>
> The dandelion just wants to be sure that every single opportunity for reproduction is exploited!...

Dandelions and artists have a lot in common in the age of the Internet. This is, of course, the age of unlimited, zero-marginal-cost copying. If you blow your works into the net like a dandelion clock on the breeze, the net itself will take care of the copying costs.[8]

It is interesting to note that it isn't what is actually popular that matters – rather: 'what people like depends on what they *think other people like*'[9] – and that various specific cultural signals show us what is popular, which is why charts like Billboard's and the *New York Times* bestseller list, and awards like the Oscars, are themselves massive drivers of increased consumption. This is why studios put so much money into Oscar promotion and why some less scrupulous cultural creators and promoters will go to even further lengths to appear in a chart, even if only for an instant. ResultSource, for example, is a marketing consultancy who specialize in getting books onto bestseller lists, for a fee.[10]

Not content

Content marketing has become something of a cause to celebrate in the advertising world since I started writing this book. The industry conversations started in this form because of the impact of digital that we have been talking about since around 2007, but that didn't really get traction until 2013. It was originally presented as a threat to the industry but I suspected rather that it would just cause evolution as we strove to find new ways to present brand ideas to audiences in new forms.

We have considered how it impacts business models, and how content works online in that context, and how advertising fits in, and suggested that shifting money into production, out of media, to make things people want to watch, might be a good idea.

Then everything got all real-time and agile and suddenly everyone had a newsroom and was a publisher. This is not a new approach, except in its alacrity. The *Guinness Book of Records* is brand content for the beer, to settle arguments in the pub. The *Michelin Guide* is brand content for the tyre company, to encourage people to drive to restaurants further afield. All original programmes on television, before spot advertising, were branded content.

Content is great, if a bit tiring if you try to keep up the pace of a newsroom, but my concern is that we just shifted from assuming advertising was the solution to all problems, to assuming content is the solution.

Trying to create content that earns attention is a good idea, but it also opens us up to being in competition for attention with an infinite amount of content, made by everyone, of different qualities, from childish to professional. The solus function of most of this content is to aggregate attention, because this is the only measure of the 'quality' of any quantum of content. If attention is scarcer and scarcer every day, brand content has to navigate all that as well, and then precipitate some commercial impact after.

Maybe it does present a threat to the creative advertising industry, since, well, our other partners, the media companies that we've been buying attention from for all these years, also have a business model problem, and are really good at making content, relatively fast, which is designed to attract attention. The internet promised to swallow the costs of reproduction and distribution – so we started thinking like dandelions, squeezing out lots of tiny pieces of content, all the time, to work into the content cadence of real people on these platforms.

The biggest challenge for marketing clients today is what, out of an ever-increasing number of options, to consider and leverage to achieve their business goals – and how to create holistic solutions that cater for increasingly diverse media/technology audiences, some of whom watch a lot of television and some of whom do not. It is surprising how entrenched and oddly recidivist some aspects of the industry have become, despite endlessly announcing their evolution. As recently as 2014, consumer-packaged goods giant Reckitt Benckiser felt the need to restructure its relationships with advertising agencies to avoid 'TV-led thinking'.[11]

Perhaps it's not that surprising. It is, after all, famously hard to get anyone to understand something, when their income depends on not understanding it. Agencies are fighting for a slice of a shrinking pie, as large clients seek to actively depress the amount of money they spend on 'non-advertising expenditures' (ie agency fees).[12] It is unlikely that agencies with separate profit and loss (P&L) are really set up to collaborate, despite the consolidated holding company promises, which, in light of the failed Publicis Omnicom merger, ring increasingly hollow.

Despite the programmatic promises of the massive media buyers, very few people outside the ad-tech and media ecosystem care about, or notice, banners. Publishers are trying to wean themselves off their click addiction and develop native branded content offerings. Search remains the key online advertising driver in dollar terms, especially on mobile.

Social media have become the battlegrounds for agency ideas, precisely because they cut across all disciplines and, unlike search, allow room for actual ideas. Advertising, media, PR, digital, CRM, activation, and any other agency that is characterized by discipline has laid claim to social – it is uniquely horizontal. Social is how content flows, how customers communicate with brands and each other, how ideas spread. When a company does something badly, or well, social is where we reach out to them, and to each other.

Social return on investment (ROI) debates rage on, but suddenly every brand seems to be creating content as though it were some kind of panacea. I suspect that this is simply because the apparatus of the advertising industry has always been set up to create pieces of 'content', although there is an important distinction here. Content is something a consumer would choose to consume. Advertising is something a brand wants to say about itself. They occasionally overlap, but rarely.

But this is not to say that broadcast television advertising, or billboards, or radio are somehow no longer present. That's salespersonship, not strategy.

Certain audiences, especially those over the age of 50, continue to consume vast swathes of real-time broadcast television as they did before. Billboards are more important than ever for cultural impact – they cannot be blocked or skipped. We also know how important radio still is – especially, for example, for Americans outside of New York – because everyone drives everywhere, to everything.

Rather, understand that all media should be considered as part of one interoperating system. Components can act upon each other in approaching real time. Eventually all elements will be digital. The definitions we cling to, such as television versus online video, make sense only in light of business model Balkanization, and only for the medium term. One-third of millennials – the generation born after 1980 – only watch 'television' on the internet, where Netflix predicts that, eventually, there will be no advertisements.[13]

It is not about what you make, but what effect you have on the system. Introducing a pervasive *effect*, not element, into this system is now the job of advertising.

And, increasingly, content alone won't be enough to do that.

PART THREE
Attention arts and sciences

Do things, tell people

How to behave in a world of infinite content

If content is no longer sufficient – what should brands do?

Previously, the ability to make things public, to publish, was a privileged act. It was expensive and hard and, in many cases, illegal. When the printing press emerged it was viewed by the status quo as a tool that should be used to support the status quo, somewhat unsurprisingly. Unlicensed printing presses were illegal in England until the end of the 17th century, as they still are in Malaysia today. When the age of mass media arrived, only governments, the media-industrial complex and the advertising industry were able to create mass culture. So, when you saw these pieces of culture, you couldn't help but be impressed.

The exponential impact of Moore's Law means that the computing power of a bespoke Silicon Graphics workstation, such as was used to create the special effects for *Terminator 2* and *Jurassic Park*, can be approximated on a laptop. In 2009, a filmmaker in Uruguay made a five-minute short called *Panic Attack* with a US $500 budget and uploaded it to YouTube.[1] It features animated robots attacking a city – and got him noticed by a Hollywood production company. No doubt there was an element of luck in this dandelion spore attracting enough attention to do so, but the fact remains that digital technology has given every consumer the power to create content. And it's getting easier. As media author Clay Shirky has pointed out, what once took an industry – publishing – now takes the press of a button on a blogging platform. The monetary power of brands no longer buys them *that* uniqueness. We can all make films and we can all create web pages. The magic that exclusive access to this technology used to deliver has evaporated.

'Content' producers – the role traditionally taken by ad agencies in the marketing industry – no longer have exclusive access to content creation. That is not to say that the quality of 'consumer generated content' (a tellingly oxymoronic term) is usually on par with Hollywood or Madison Avenue. Rather, the gap between not being able to do something and being able to do it is infinite, but the gap between being bad and excellent is simply one of degree.

It is hard to be amazed with any technical wizardry on film when you grow up with iMovie at your fingertips. The web provides a mechanism that can absorb the cost of distribution. Advertising, or even content, as the sole tool in the marketing box, is simply no longer sufficient to earn attention since it now competes with practically infinite volumes of content created by people. The mass media has been forced to make room for the media of the masses in the attention market.

Some advertising agencies have attempted to reposition themselves in the new world, shunning the word advertising, expanding their remit to become purveyors of ideas providing solutions to business problems. And indeed, they could and perhaps even should be, as we will discuss later in this chapter, but expanding this definition of advertising needs different skills and, perhaps, a different lens through which to understand the world.

Historically, the function of an advertising agency was seen as expressing, through art and copy, truths about the product or the company in the most compelling way. Brand informs the advertising (Figure 6.1). As the most visible aspect of a company, it was only mistrusted when it directly contravened a customer's personal experience of the said company. As we have seen, this is no longer the case. Any dissonance between promises and delivery experienced by anyone – and then shared – erodes trust in the brand in totality. Cumulatively, this has eroded trust in brands and advertising overall.

FIGURE 6.1   Traditional brand platform informs advertising

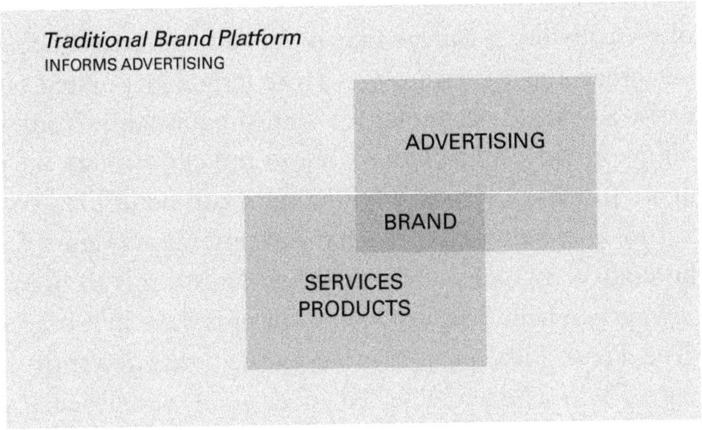

This dissonance is equally exposed through social media, as every employee of the company becomes a hole in the semi-permeable membrane of the corporate communication department, and content, as brands look to find things to talk about beyond endless exhortations to buy.

Douglas Rushkoff suggests this requires the abandoning of communications 'as some separate task, and instead just doing all the right things that you want talked about'.[2] Brands will be built by behaviour... and content that communicates that behaviour.

Behaviour, actions at scale, can be a continuing role for marketing and their agency partners. Brands must become behavioural templates, driving the action of the company, which should be expressed through actions and initiatives designed to earn attention.

There are things that corporations and their agencies partners can do that cannot be easily replicated by individuals, which do not rely on them being vertically integrated. They still have strategic advantages in the quest for attention: technology and scale. In a world of infinite content, actions created at scale can become content engines. Do things in the world, then tell people.

Technology is a medium

Technology provides a canvas that is yet to be effectively colonized by the amateur and, as Arthur C. Clarke famously pointed out, any sufficiently advanced technology is indistinguishable from magic. Technology provides a medium to amaze and cut through the clutter of content. Technology speaks by doing, it can be utilized to create utilities, tools, services and ideas that earn attention (Figure 6.2).

Technology companies often tout their latest tools to brands and media owners to help drive uptake, so brands have first user advantages. The Pepsi TEN project is an explicit manifestation of this advantage. The consumer-packaged goods giant established a venture fund to support and partner with early stage technology start-ups in order to exclusively leverage the technologies for marketing.

There are problems with the blurring of the technology and the communications industries. They are divided by a common language. Words that should mean the same thing can mean something completely different to those on either side of the divide.

FIGURE 6.2   Integrative brand platform

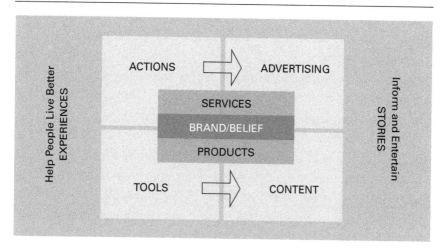

SOURCE: Genius Steals

Take a simple word like *platform*. To a communications specialist it means an idea or theme that all messages fit into, but to a technologist it means an underlying technology that enables other products or services to be built on it. This means that collaboration among disciplines can seem to be aligned when it isn't.

In practice, creative directors trained in writing or design find themselves being asked to review algorithms and concepts they cannot understand, as code becomes a creative deliverable.

CASE STUDY

The World Wildlife Fund (WWF) briefed their agency for a campaign to promote the saving of trees by being more cautious about office printing – the paperless office never having emerged. Jung Von Matt realized pretty quickly that a traditional ad campaign – especially a print campaign, for obvious reasons – wasn't the right solution. Instead they worked for years to develop a bespoke file format, similar to the popular Adobe pdf format, which simply could not be printed. Technology here speaks volumes. The idea is a tool, something people can use, which makes the brand idea useful to its audience.

For brands to take advantage of technology and their first-access rights to new developments, they and their agents need to develop common understanding.

Often it is the role of the strategist to translate business language into creative inspiration. Increasingly, additional translations are necessary, evinced by the formation of new agency roles, reverse mentoring, and the demand for management training from groups such as the HyperIsland digital school.

There have been significant difficulties in merging the culture of advertising and digital agencies. Dare was named the digital agency of the decade in the UK by *Campaign* magazine. Advertising agency MCBD was named Effectiveness Agency of the year by the IPA. In 2010 they merged and it was heralded as an excellent idea, creating a new model agency that understood the narrative of advertising with the participatory and technology nous required for innovative interactive work. Unfortunately, it faltered and became emblematic of 'the story of an industry that knew it had to change, but didn't really know how; or, for that matter, what to change into'.[3]

The newly formed agency struggled with developing an appropriate process to manage such disparate outputs. It struggled to convince clients that a full service offering was feasible or desirable. But it struggled most with one of the key problems of all mergers, the integration of culture. John Owen, head of strategy at Dare, later went on to write that he had come to believe that this sort of cultural fusion was impossible, because: 'when it comes to culture, the choice is binary: you can be digital or you can be advertising'. He goes on to explain how traditional advertising agencies so often still think and how it differs from digitally born agencies:

So what do I mean by a digital culture?

I mean not insisting on creative director sign-off for everything and elevating the role of the creative team above all other disciplines in the idea-generation phase. I mean empowering multidisciplinary teams to work in fast, fluid ways, with different people taking the lead depending on the nature of the brief.[4]

This cultural mismatch is not just about process. It leads to endless, pointless, arguments about the death of advertising, or the impact of digital, or who owns the idea, or who is lead agency – each agency defending their own business model and place at the table. It moves the industry further away from the integrative marketing communications planning that is needed in this environment. The fragmentation of marketing solutions is why, according to a survey of chief marketing officers, integration is the most important thing they want from their agencies and among the top reasons that they pick or dismiss them.[5]

The field of user experience design looks at enhancing customer satisfaction and loyalty by improving the usability and pleasure in the interactions between customers and products or services. Some see this as bridging the gap between product design and traditional marketing. Mapping a consumer journey, their step-by-step experience of a product or service, is a tool that has been adopted by communication planners dealing with the complexity of the modern landscape.

CASE STUDY

Airline Virgin America revamped its web storefront to make using it more intuitive across different devices, with a focus on making the arduous task of booking travel easier and faster. Booking travel is increasingly complex, due to the number of options available and the dynamic pricing models of the industry. Research by the Boston Consulting Group suggests that a customer spends, on average, 42 hours online to research, plan and book a four-day trip, which is both staggering and unpleasant.[6] So, faster and easier is a huge boon and the Virgin brand is further bolstered by its other stated ambition for the site: to make every task 'fun-erer'.[7]

Actions at scale

Brands still have an advantage over empowered consumers – their ability to deliver scale. Ironically this can be most powerful when delivered in traditional broadcast media environments because consumers cannot access them directly, as they can with online environments.

Digital channels may now deliver massive reach but the almost infinite nature of the web means that individual elements can lack the cultural impact of television and the associated media that reports on it. Fragmentation leads to the counter-intuitive fact that things can be incredibly popular on the internet and yet you and I may never hear about them.

CASE STUDY

Doritos' Crash the Super Bowl campaign is a classic example of using scale. Leveraging the consumer's ability to make films Doritos then incentivizes them to participate by giving them the opportunity to see their ad in the biggest TV event of the year. The campaign has been running for seven years. (Longevity is another sign of a powerful idea in a world of accelerating news cycles and diminished attention spans.)

Scale can be delivered via access. Tablets and laptops, for all their ability to democratize the creation of content, will not get you close to the big stars, although Twitter disrupts even this advantage. Brands can leverage their corporate might to provide access to things that an individual's money cannot buy. Coca-Cola experimented with this when they sponsored a live online recording session with the band Maroon 5. The band composed and recorded a track, aided by feedback and suggestions from people in real time.

In the age of the empowered consumer, brands need to identify what they can do that consumers cannot, how they can add something to their lives. Technology may be part of the answer, if brands and technologists can learn to speak the same language, but it could also be via the appropriate actions at scale that gives consumers something that even the latest laptop, tablet or mobile cannot offer.

Scale can be utilized to do things so far beyond the scope of individuals that it generates content that is truly awe inspiring. In October 2012, energy drink Red Bull created one of the greatest marketing actions of all time. It was called Stratos,[8] and consisted of skydiver Felix Baumgartner breaking the world free-fall record by jumping out of a capsule suspended 24 miles above the surface of the earth. A project seven years in the making, it captured the attention of the world. As he plummeted earthward, reaching speeds in excess of 800 miles an hour, the jump was broadcast on more than 40 television stations across 50 countries. A record 8 million people watched it live on YouTube. It organically created more than 2.5 million social media mentions, front page news worth millions of dollars and immediately became a cultural object. It has been suggested that it is the 'most successful marketing campaign of all time', indelibly linked to the Red Bull brand and its long-running slogan 'Red Bull Gives You Wings'. On the one-year anniversary of the jump, Red Bull released a secondary burst of content, including a powerful point-of-view video of Felix's experience.

Acts of happiness

Whilst actions that are epic in scale such as Stratos are awesome, smaller actions that make real people happy in the real world can also be very effective at generating attention.

CASE STUDY

Coca-Cola has very successfully championed this model, creating a series of video vignettes about very surprising vending machines. Beginning in 2010, Coca-Cola wanted to find ways to reach teens through social media, understanding that content is not searched for but shared. As a global brand manager explained, they 'wanted to give [fans] something that would spread a bit of happiness and something they could pass on to their friends to keep the happiness flowing'.[9] The most successful element of this digital campaign was footage of an activation that had been set up at St John's University, a private school in Queens, New York. An ordinary-looking Coca-Cola vending machine was installed in the cafeteria and surreptitiously filmed. (One assumes that the people involved signed releases once all was revealed.) Unsuspecting students would go up to the machine, put in some money to buy a Coca-Cola, but the machine dispensed happiness instead – in the form of surprise gifts, such as a 6-foot-long sandwich, a bouquet of flowers, 20 bottles of Coca-Cola or a pizza. The students were clearly surprised and delighted, and because the gifts came in large quantities, they shared them. Their reactions were charming and clearly real – and *real* things done in the *real* world to *real* people seem to have increased impact in a digitally driven world. (It used to be the 'Real Thing', remember?)

The film cost about $50,000, a fraction of the cost of a broadcast advertisement, and achieved significant organic reach, viewed more than 6 million times on YouTube. Viewers from all over the world saw and shared it, and it was eventually used on television, reversing the traditional direction of advertising, from television to online (which is, as we shall see later, the way things should usually be done). It spawned a whole series of similar activations, all of which performed well and all of which imparted some aspect of shared happiness.

Another, very different, kind of action helped Coca-Cola to express that drinks are better shared. They created a can that splits in two so that you can literally share a can.

Platforms and products

Let's go back to that term that gets used to mean so many different things: platform. A new definition of this term, at the intersection of business and technology, had begun to manifest by 2014. Platforms, when understood as the 'rules and infrastructure that facilitate interactions among network users'[10] have been hailed as the future of marketing by Adrian Ho, one of the founders of Zeus Jones, a new model agency from Minneapolis. It built on the idea that the definition of a brand had evolved from a construct of messaging and perception, to a guiding principle that create 'experiences and communities centered on a core purpose'.[11] As they say: 'if platforms are the future of business then brands aren't just a way to describe "what you do," they are a way to describe "what we can do together".'[12]

CASE STUDY

The Nikon Film Festival was an early attempt I worked on to create a platform that enabled brands and people to work together. Nikon had been running a successful series of television commercials featuring Ashton Kutcher. I had recently joined McCann New York to help them think about the impact of digital, blessed with the baroque title Executive Vice President Chief Technology Strategist (there was a concern that the more usual title of Chief Digital Officer might upset some creative directors). We got a new brief for the newly launching Nikon D5000, their first Digital SLR camera that could shoot HD film.

The CEO of Nikon at the time was very fond of Ashton. The client briefed us in for yet another TV spot featuring Kutcher, to launch a new camera that could record HD moving pictures. I begged them to let us develop an online film festival instead, based on the far from ground-breaking insight that people who might specifically want a camera that shot HD film might be interested in shooting HD film.

This was in 2009 and Twitter had just popped into the popular consciousness thanks to the race to be the first to reach 1 million followers, a race that was won by none other than Kutcher. Thus, an idea began to coalesce, and I managed to convince the CEO that we should do a film festival, built around Twitter and its impact on media, and have Kutcher kick it off by actually making a film, rather than pretending to in an advertisement.

I explained to the CEO that Twitter was indeed 'cool' when he asked, and he gave us his blessing. This is one of the great things about having the CEO as the client, they can just sign off on things by themselves. What good CEOs are usually best at is making decisions (and then selling those decisions to the market).

The festival launched with a Tweet from Kutcher sharing his film and directing others to post a film that showed 'a day through their lens' in 140 seconds, echoing the character limit of Twitter, for a top prize of $100,000. With that much money at stake, we were hoping we would get a lot of high-quality entries, but we were staggered by the response. We received more than 48 hours of film, with a huge range of ideas. There was a round of voting, followed by a panel of judges, so each contestant was out there trying to promote their own films hard through their social channels. This is one of the keys of social engagement, inspiring individuals to promote and propagate your brand idea to their networks.

After millions of views, winners were chosen and awarded. Here's where the story gets a little sad. We had built a new film format and platform to host it and a community coalesced around it. But back then we were still operating in the mindset of traditional advertising, of campaigns that start and then finish, not platforms that provide ongoing value and communication opportunities for the brand and the community. So, once the campaign was over, the site came down.

However, this story has an unexpected happy ending. While working on this book in France, I Googled the project to look at some of the press coverage and, thanks to localized search, discovered that the French Nikon team had also used the idea and were still running the film festival and web platform five years later. A platform that provides persistent value for participants.

Recombinant culture
Talent imitates, genius steals

> *Everything is destined to reappear as simulation. Landscapes as photography, women as the sexual scenario, thoughts as writing, terrorism as fashion and the media, events as television.*
>
> *Things seem only to exist by the virtue of this strange destiny. You wonder whether the world itself isn't just here to serve as advertising copy in some other world.*
>
> **JEAN BAUDRILLARD**

I believe that ideas are new combinations. I believe that stealing is genius, but copying is the reserve of the uninspired.

I believe originality is a romantic notion, often depicted as Athena springing forth fully formed from the mind of Zeus, and just as mythical. When something is perceived as original, what we mean is that it is unexpected, novel to that person, not that is has no antecedents.

I believe, like the postmodernists, that you can attempt to create a higher order of meaning by standing on the semantic foundations of other creations, employing referents instead of starting from scratch.

I believe that the remix is the dominant cultural construct of a digital age, bits endlessly co-mingling with bits.

The idea of the remix can be traced back at least as far as the philosopher John Locke. Back in the 17th century, he posited that human imagination was a sampler and sequencer – cutting and pasting perceived reality into new constructs.

All ideas work like this. The archeology of any idea involves decompiling it into its constituent elements. Creating ideas is the same process reversed:

- Jonah Lehrer points out in *How We Decide* (2009) that 'from the perspective of the brain – new ideas are just several old ideas had at the same time'.[1]

- Stephen Johnson, in *Where Good Ideas Come From* (2010), has explored the notion that only some ideas are possible at any moment – he calls this solution space the 'adjacent possible'.[2]

The most obvious combinations, the most obvious ideas and the most obvious creative solutions to a brief sit at the nearest edge of the adjacent possible. This is why the first round of responses to the same brief tend to be so similar, again and again. This is why so many ideas are the same, copying, either conscious or unconscious, blending with convergent evolution, as minds tackle the same problems in different places.

How, then, to have better ideas? Better, more unusual, more interesting, more differentiating ideas exist at the furthest viable extremes of the adjacent possible (Figure 7.1).

So, in order to get them you must:

- Expose yourself to the most diverse set of influences possible, and allow luck to lead you.

- Get past all the obvious ideas first.

Ideas are new combinations

Being creative is not a magical skill, it is simply a way of thinking, a process, one that combines things in non-obvious ways in order to achieve something useful or beautiful or both.

FIGURE 7.1 Good ideas are non-obvious, non-trivial combinations

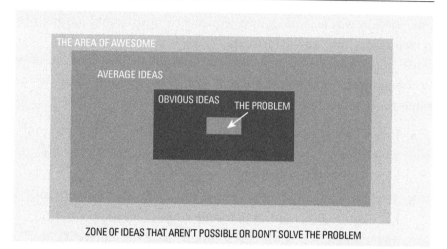

SOURCE: Genius Steals

When someone remarks on how creative something is, it is usually because the combination is particularly non-obvious to the person making the remark. The combination has to work, somehow, has to find the similarity that holds the two disparate ideas together. Finding the connection between two disparate things is the flash, the eureka moment of insight, the feeling of having an idea.

This is why Aristotle thought that 'the greatest thing by far is to have a command of metaphor',[3] because you have to be able to find similarity in difference. Metaphors are the heart of thoughts, of new ideas. Remember, even memories, engrams, are being remixed and remade every time they are recalled. This is why, when James Webb Young sat down to write a technique for producing ideas, he expressed quite clearly that '*ideas are new combinations*'.

Innovative ideas are associative: 'What the innovators have in common is that they can put together ideas and information in unique combinations that nobody else has quite put together before.'[4] Researchers describe this ability to connect ideas as 'associating', and believe 'it is key to innovators' ability' to create non-obvious combinations.[5]

Crucially, finding non-obvious connections tends to mean that the mind doing the mixing has knowledge of concepts in areas that are not *directly* adjacent.

Let's go back to John Locke and his essay concerning human understanding. Locke is the godfather of remix culture. He set out to establish a model of the human mind and understand where ideas come from, essentially as a direct response to *innatism*, which suggested ideas are in your mind when you are born. Locke wanted to apply the newly scientific principles of empiricism to the mind, rather than relying on superstition. He hoped to develop a more robust epistemology of science, by examining the limitations, reliability and scope of the human mind. The idea he came to, his most famous image, was describing the mind as being, originally, a *tabula rasa*.

(Suggesting that all minds were born blank had an obvious political analogue: that all men are born equal. Indeed, Locke's work had a profound impact on the thinking and writing of the founding fathers of the United States. Several sections of the Declaration of Independence are stolen almost verbatim from Locke.)

If minds are blank, where then do ideas come from? You steal them.

Ronald Burt's theory of 'where to get a good idea' helps to explain that it is probably stolen: 'The usual image of creativity is that it's some sort of genetic gift, some heroic act, but creativity is an import–export game. It's not a creation game.'[6] It is the act of transposing something onto a new frame of reference that often renders it valuable: 'The trick is, can you get an idea which is mundane and well-known in one place to another place where people would get value out of it?'[7]

Burt's line of enquiry stretches back at least as far as Locke, who wanted to understand where ideas come from, although he had a broader definition of idea in mind – essentially the object of any thought. His answer was from *sensation* and *reflection*. Simple ideas are experienced directly by the senses – horse, for example – and then we use our mental facility to combine them to build more complex, abstract ideas – take a horn and a horse and you've got a unicorn, even though you have never encountered one in real life.

All ideas are iterative and accretive, built on that which came before. Your imagination is a remix engine, and the less obvious the working remix, the more tension between the pieces, the more 'creative' the idea seems to us.

This is why, to quote Burt again: 'People who live in the intersection of social worlds, are at higher risk of having good ideas.' So being a bridge among different groups, exposing yourself to lots of difference, is necessary but not sufficient for having ideas.

The *tabula rasa* idea finds its antecedent in an Aristotelian maxim: 'there is nothing in the intellect that was not previously in the senses'.[8] This was built upon hundred of years later by Leibniz, in reference to Locke's usage, to include 'except the intellect itself'.[9] Your unique idea engine can take the same sources as the person next to you and come up with something different, which is the infinite novelty of *recombinant thinking*, but also reminds that you have to exercise the creative faculty, learning and combining.

Art is one way of doing this.

Great artists steal

Men nearly always follow the tracks made by others and proceed in their affairs by imitation, even though they cannot entirely keep to the tracks of others or emulate the prowess of their models. So a prudent man should always follow in the footsteps of great men and imitate those who have been outstanding. If his own prowess fails to compare with theirs, at least it has an air of greatness about it.

THE PRINCE, NICCOLÒ MACHIAVELLI

Banksy steals great art and becomes a greater artist:

CASE STUDY

In June 2009, the English graffiti prankster and self-styled 'art terrorist' known only as Banksy had his first official exhibition in Bristol.

Banksy's previous displays in art galleries had been guerrilla incursions – illegally installed pieces designed, at least in part, to deride the elitist exclusivity of the environments.

The pieces themselves are part of a larger process – the surreptitious hanging, the context, all combine to create the meanings that Banksy wishes to manufacture.

In March 2005, disguised as a British pensioner, in raincoat and fake beard, he 'donated' pieces to four museums in New York on the same day. Each piece was a remix, a comment on the work in that museum. At the Museum of Modern Art he left behind a soup can, styled on Warhol's own endlessly replicated *Campbell's Soup Cans*, but drawing its cultural cues from the UK supermarket Tesco. (The name Tesco is itself a mash-up of the founder's first supplier, TE Stockwell, and his surname Cohen. It is usually claimed to have been a mash-up of his wife's name, Tessa, and their surname, but Lady Cohen's name was Sarah.)

In May 2005 Banksy hit the British Museum, leaving behind a 'cave painting' that denoted 'a stick man chasing a wildebeest and pushing a shopping cart', attributed to 'Banksymus Maximus' in Gallery 49. (The British Museum later added the piece to its permanent collection, creating, in effect, an anti-theft.)

When invited to put on a legal exhibit at Bristol's City Museum and Art Gallery, Banksy's response was characteristically irreverent and referential. Riffing off his earlier covert museum work, this show was put together in semi-secret and took the sensibility of graffiti to the gallery.

Graffiti can be considered the inverse of found art. In found art, the *objet trouvé* is removed from its normal surroundings and, recontextualized by the artist – such as the urinal becomes a fountain – it becomes 'readymade' art. Street art takes the opposite approach – it is the canvas that is *found* and, through illegal daubing and stencilled slogans, the world becomes the gallery.

Banksy's work in particular makes dynamic use of context. When he spray-painted 'This is not a photo opportunity' at various picturesque locations, he encompassed the whole landscape, and subverted the old Kodak signage that attempted to do the same.

So when given a gallery in which to exhibit, it was perhaps inevitable that the gallery, that art itself, would become the canvas. Many of his pieces were, in effect, graffiti on other pieces of art: remixes. The title of the show pays testament to this: it was called *Banksy versus Bristol Museum*. Referencing the naming convention of soundclashes and mash-ups, Banksy's entire show was a remix of the Bristol Museum.

And with one sculpture in particular, he acknowledged his role as part of our unending culture of *recombinance*. On a stone slab, he engraved a quotation (attributed to Pablo Picasso):

THE BAD ARTISTS IMITATE, THE GREAT ARTISTS STEAL

He signed it *Pablo Picasso* and then scrawled out his name and scratched 'Banksy' beneath.

Banksy stole the idea and made it his own, volunteering himself for inclusion in the canon of great artists. The show was one of the top 30 most visited exhibitions in the world in 2009 – the first time the Bristol Museum has ever appeared on the list. The incredible success of the show is testament not only to Banksy's meteoric rise but also the increased saliency of recombinant culture.

Same same but different

Warhol took the idea of iterative artwork and productized it. He applied Ford's manufacturing model to the business of art. As John Cale, who founded The Velvet Underground with Lou Reed, once said: 'it wasn't called the Factory for nothing. It was where the assembly line for the silkscreens happened.'[10]

Warhol was unashamedly recombinant. The Pop Art movement was predicated on the democratization of art through the reappropriation of popular culture: *Pop* is short for popular. His production line churned out endless variants of the same silkscreens, each the same but slightly different. He mass-produced art, echoing the mass media and mass market that sprang into existence in the 1950s and 1960s. (Later in his career he collaborated with Jean-Michel Basquiat, letting the young art-world celebrity remix his beloved prints.)

Warhol's repetitive production-line style called into question the image of the artist as divinely inspired genius, or even as craftsperson. It called into question the sanctity of originality, and he delighted in this blasphemy, boasting about his minimal involvement in his work and his army of assistants. His *Do It Yourself* series of paintings, based on popular painting-by-numbers kits, further explored this idea.

Even within single works, Warhol explores the idea of versions and iteration, creating multi-image quadtychs of celebrities such as Elvis Presley, Marilyn Monroe (and, inevitably for the master of self-branding, himself) and of even more famous things, namely packaged goods: Campbell's Soup and Coca-Cola.

These multi-chromatic quadtychs became one of the defining creative frameworks of the Pop Art movement, which have been endlessly reiterated since. To promote a Warhol retrospective Tate Modern, in partnership with agencies Naked Communications and Poke London, created a *Warholizer* on their website. It let anyone upload a photo of themselves and turned it into a colourful quadtych, which was then displayed for 15 minutes on the Tate Modern homepage – giving participants their 15 minutes, and megabytes, of fame: 'We like to think that perhaps this is the kind of thing that Andy might have done if he'd had computers and stuff. Sort of like a modern-day factory.'[11]

That was in 2002. Since then, the tools of content production, manipulation and distribution have changed dramatically – for the simpler. Today, if someone wants to create a Warholized self-portrait and have it displayed online they need only to launch the Photobooth application on a Macbook – it has a 'Pop Art' effect that will automatically turn a picture captured on the embedded iSight camera into a multicoloured quadtych – snap a picture and upload it.

Warhol's work has inspired countless reproductions of its reproductions. In a thoroughly modern expression of inspiration, Ken Solomon painted a watercolour of the Google Image Search results page for the keyword 'Warhol' – re-aggregating the disparate Warholian pieces according to the ranking of the Google algorithm, which is dictated in large part by the number of links each image has to it.

Warhol was a branding genius, very consciously turning himself into an art brand. He was not doing this just to appease his childhood insecurities (although that was probably part of it). It was because he approached art as a business: 'Making money is art and working is art and good business is the best art.'[12]

In his book – *The Philosophy of Andy Warhol* – he makes the branding point even more explicitly. He talks about being jealous of 'Levi and Strauss. I wish I could invent something like blue jeans. Something to be remembered for. Something mass.'[13]

This is a wonderful sentiment – art not for the elite but for everyone – but also very commercially minded. It is echoed in a quote from Posh Spice – who said she wanted to be 'as famous as Persil' – as Jeremy Bullmore pointed out.[14] Packaged-goods brands are more famous than any celebrity will ever be.

All POPular artists understand that the value of any work of art, like the value of a brand, is entirely socially created – it only has value because we agree that it does. Which means that the entire art industry is predicated on a very simple value equation: people will pay more for something people have paid attention to.

People will pay more for something people have paid attention to

Correspondingly, the more people have heard of the artist and his or her work, the more it is worth. So the business of art is fame, to become popular, to make itself famous, to create brands, to attract attention. As you may have guessed, I think this mechanism underlies a lot of culture, especially advertising.

Advertising is not art. Advertising agencies are not in the business of making cool stuff, they are in the business of making money for clients, using creativity. That said, successful art is also very commercially minded, by definition, since success ultimately is measured by the prices an artist can sell their work for. This is not, perhaps, aesthetic success, but if the perfect piece of art lies somewhere, forever unseen, its impact on culture is assumed to be limited.

In a world where mainstream media is increasingly supplemented by the media of the masses, one of the leverage points for creativity is earning attention, beyond that which has been paid for. This means that, as with art, part of the business of advertising is fame, at least among the desired customer base.

Modern postmodernism

In which we look at what was stolen from postmodernism.

The idea that 'Talent Imitates, [but] Genius Steals' has been, in recombinant fashion, attributed to various different people, in various different forms. Morrissey used it as the title of one of his albums, in a form attributed to Oscar Wilde: *Talent Borrows, Genius Steals*. The Picasso version that Banksy appropriated is among the most famous, but it is also attributed to TS Eliot, in the form of 'good poets borrow, great poets steal'.

In fact, none of them seem to have said it, exactly, but like the recombinant idea it has been endlessly reiterated and put into the mouths of authorities.

The *fauxtation* seems to be derived from something that Eliot did write, however, in a piece published in his collection of criticism, *The Sacred Wood* (1920). In his essay on Elizabethan dramatist Philip Massinger, Eliot attempts to establish some grounds upon which to judge his work, or any work, and so in turn judge the judgements. An earlier critic, Alfred Cruickshank, suggested that Massinger's work was 'inferior', partially at least because it was perceived to be derivative. To which Eliot responds: 'One of the surest of tests is the way in which a poet borrows. Immature poets imitate; mature poets steal... A good poet will usually borrow from authors remote in time, or alien in language, or diverse in interest.'[15]

With his usual precision, Eliot captures a crucial component of the postmodern view of culture, one that continues to echo throughout our increasingly digital mediascape, and makes clear the distinction between copying and stealing. Imitation defaces, stealing makes something better, 'or at least something different'. The key is that something else is created, something 'new'.

When genius steals, a new whole is created, not simply a mismatched bricolage. There is communication between the disparate elements, which add to the whole. Stealing from remote sources – in time, language or interest – adds to the dynamic tension being created between the elements, but the broader the sources, the harder it can be to create cohesion among them.

This is why the consultancy I founded with my wife is called *Genius Steals*. It is built on what we believe about innovation. We look to the broadest range of sources when we help to craft solutions for our clients – and build from them, rather than starting from scratch.

Imitation disguises the debt it owes. Stealing takes and repurposes, recontextualizes – it revels in the reference. Recognizing the source becomes an integral part of the meaning being constructed. In this sense, stealing is hypertextual and meta-textual – it links to other texts outside itself, standing on the semantic foundations previously established.

Stealing multiplies meaning, copying does not.

Postmodernism posits culture as a self-conscious stock house of signs. The insight that words had no inherent relationship to the concepts they denote cleaved signifier from signified. Since meaning is impossible to definitively assign, texts pull established signifiers into service as referents:

> Thanks to the processes which led to postmodernism, all culture is a buffet table. It is not so much what the chef prepares but what the diner puts together as his or her meal that counts; appropriation is an act of creativity. Because everything is in quotes in postmodernism, the allusion may be the most important literary device of our age.[16]

Postmodernism is considered by some to be a reaction to, or assimilation of, our intensely mediated culture. Postmodernism questions the foundations of cultural and artistic forms through self-referential irony and the juxtaposition of elements from popular culture and technology.

Digital culture is increasingly postmodern in this sense – cultural artefacts are made up of allusions, references and quotations. Eliot himself was pre-postmodern, but modernism was also concerned with exploring the multiplicity of different viewpoints – his masterpiece *The Waste Land* was originally titled *He Do The Police In Different Voices* – that recombination offers, and the extensive use of quotation, allusion and reference, which brought up the perennial question of plagiarism: is it imitation or stealing? On this point:

> Eliot evidenced no small anxiety about these matters; the notes he so carefully added to *The Waste Land* can be read as a symptom of modernism's contamination anxiety. Taken from this angle, what exactly is postmodernism, except modernism without the anxiety?[17]

This lack of anxiety about stealing typifies postmodern and today's thinking. An understanding that everything that came before is contained in the works of the present is fundamental to a postmodern understanding of art, culture, technology and innovation. The technologies that are changing our world are themselves built on endless iteration and recombination from within, and inspiration from without. Steve Jobs, arguably one of the principal architects of the emerging mediascape thanks to innovations such as iTunes, the iPhone and the iPad, has always been clear about the need to steal:

Ultimately it comes down to taste. It comes down to trying to expose yourself to the best things that humans have done and then try to bring those things in to what you're doing... we have always been shameless about stealing great ideas.[18]

Steve goes on to outline some of the key elements of creative thinking:

- *Iteration*: building on what came before, looking at what works and starting there, rather than from scratch.

- *Recombination*: blending different elements together to create a new whole.

- *Inspiration*: looking to fields 'diverse in interest' for sources to recombine.

The development of media technologies in the last two decades that enable the instantaneous and simple reproduction of content have facilitated the emergence of a generation of idea prosumers (a term denoting a blend of producer and consumer, first coined by Alvin Toffler) for whom remixing is the default way to express themselves. Normalized by habitual usage of control+C and control+V shortcuts on their keyboard, a cut'n'paste generation has emerged for whom pre-existing media products are as colours on a palette.

The tools required to manufacture meaning have been put into the hands of a whole generation, and their primary mode of expression is postmodern: allusion and quotation, samples and soundbites – they remix culture to create it.

But this free and easy remixing of culture is not simply a function of the times, or technologies. Whilst it seems that this recombinant culture is just dawning, it is merely a renaissance. Modern media technologies are simply shedding light on what is a much more fundamental idea – that culture is, that all ideas are, inherently recombinant and that it cannot be otherwise.

Combination tools

How to have ideas: a genius steals process

> *And as imagination bodies forth*
> *The forms of things unknown, the poet's pen*
> *Turns them to shapes and gives to airy nothing*
> *A local habitation and a name.*
> **A MIDSUMMER NIGHT'S DREAM (ACT V, SCENE 1), WILLIAM SHAKESPEARE**

Since, somewhat unusually, I have worked as both a planner and as a creative director, I have a bilateral view of the strategic idea-creation process that is at least one half of the heart of the advertising agency offering (the other half being the management of implementation and orchestration).

I want to build on James Webb Young's technique for producing ideas, exploring more of the elements that lead to the 'A-Ha' moment, in order to make the mechanics of having ideas easier for everyone. As legendary adman Jay Chiat once said: 'creative is not a department'.[1] Advertising creatives of various flavours have specific craft skills that are very valuable, but conflating that with having ideas, which should be the dominion of everyone at a creative company and indeed everyone else, diminishes us.

The Genius Steals creative process is broken down into six steps, as set out below.

1. Define the problem

The greatest challenge to any thinker is stating the problem in a way that will allow a solution.

(ATTRIBUTED TO GEORGE BERNARD SHAW BUT PROBABLY A *FAUXTATION*)

Creative ideas in advertising exist to solve problems, usually specific business problems. The ideas must address the drivers and/or barriers to business growth in some fashion. The foundation of any solution is how the problem is defined. The application of creative thinking begins here, with the formulation, because how you define a problem determines if and how you can solve it.

A good problem statement needs to encapsulate the issue and objective, and inspire the appropriate solution. It should avoid jargon and be phrased to be as generative as possible. There is a famous and probably apocryphal story of a Toyota executive who asked his teams to brainstorm 'ways to increase their productivity'. This proved unfruitful, until he rephrased it as 'ways to make your job easier', which led to many, many suggestions.

Creating behavioural objectives can help to focus ideas. Will Collin, one of the founders of Naked, explains it well. He pointed out that the business objective might be to sell 15 per cent more mayonnaise but that phrasing it as 'getting people to try mayo on their fries'[2] will be far more inspirational for creating solutions.

2. Frame the metaphor, extract the abstraction, look for patterns

Our brains think in metaphors, in connections, and often the best ideas are patterns that have been established elsewhere that are matched onto the problem at hand. In order to do this, we have to abstract things out of the specific into the general, and where else these patterns may have been implemented. This framing then allows for the next stage, finding the right inspiration and *outspiration*, from different times, places, categories and so on.

3. Iteration, inspiration and outspiration

The components of new ideas are always other ideas. I think of them as pieces of Lego. You can make anything out of Lego, but in order to make specific things, you need specific pieces. Looking at the most successful attempts to solve similar pattern problems in the past is the first place to look for ideas that can be evolved or iterated.

Finding the right inspiration, the right Lego, is a crucial and ongoing part of any creative process. It is an adage in advertising that you must look outside advertising for inspiration. This is both true and not true.

As professionals it behoves us to be aware of the best work that is happening in our field, and the award shows make this easy for us. (This is part of their value, as we shall explore in Chapter 9.) This is inspiration. That said, we obviously want a much larger gene, or Lego, pool than this so we need stimulus from further fields: art, technology, design – all of culture is open and available online.

In genetic engineering, the process of introducing unrelated genetic material into an organism or breeding line is called outcrossing. It increases genetic diversity, therefore reducing the probability of being subject to disease or genetic abnormalities. This is why I call inspiration from outside *outspiration*. Every weird thing you are interested in, every niche of culture you geek about, is part of your stock house. Based on the abstraction, the pattern discerned in stage 2, you can begin to select and compile appropriate outspiration.

The point, again, is to find elements diverse in field and interest to apply to the problem. Outspiration can also come from inside the world of advertising, by looking at similar problems from very different categories or cultures.

The 'apple' game is a good way to get the iterative creative juices flowing (and to avoid hackneyed phrases like 'creative juices flowing', except possibly in relation to fruit-based creativity games). Divide a piece of paper into boxes, one for each member of the team or group. Everyone must draw something in each box to the brief 'apple', with the only other condition being that you cannot repeat anything already drawn. By pushing things endlessly, soon the obvious apples give way to more metaphorical interpretations of the brief, more creative iterations.

4. Recombination: blend and blend again

This is the forge, where ideas are smelted from disparate pieces. Every creation begins as a connection. Almost all brainstorm and creativity tools focus on stimulating non-obvious connections to see if they crystallize into ideas.

Naturally creatively minded people make these more obscure connections more naturally, but it is a process that everyone can be guided through, and a faculty that gets better the more you use it. Using the elements gathered above, every idea and piece of inspiration or outspiration, you can create a very simple combination engine by writing them all on separate cards and shuffling them, or laying them out on a table and seeing if you can connect two cards together into a new idea:

- *Random input*: this can be added into the mix, by simply selecting them from a dictionary and force-fitting them to the elements at hand.

- *A–Z ideas*: volume can be mustered with the A–Z game, where you create an idea for each letter of the alphabet in a short time.

- *Write in silence*: another volume driver, get everyone to write down their ideas privately for five minutes before any discussion or team brainstorming.

- *Reverse brainstorming*: looks for patterns in the negatives, looking through the antonym lens. Take the problem definition and reverse it. Instead of 'How can we solve this?', ask 'How could we cause it or make it worse?' Rather than 'What's the best idea?', ask 'What's the worst possible thing we could do?'; 'How could we create the opposite to what we want?' Use this to stimulate ideas, which can then be reversed to look for actual solutions.

5. Incubation: stop thinking, distract yourself, get out of your groove

Every creative process has this element. Once you or a team have forced your collective minds at a problem for some time, you begin to create ruts for your thinking as you move towards articulating a solution. This is when you should take a break and, importantly, think of other things. The classic bathtub eureka moment, the long brisk walk, the moment in the shower, the advice to sleep on it – these are all specifics for this general step.

When your brain stops actively working for a while, other more random connections start to get made by the combination engine of your imagination. Distracting your conscious mind, having a few drinks perhaps, suppresses the internal censor that stops some ideas coming to mind.

6. Articulation and judgement: is it good? Will it blend further? How is it to be articulated?

Ideas are fragile, the best must be protected beyond gestation or they wither and die. Once the most fruitful ideas are selected, based on how well they seem to solve the problem and how non-obvious they are, the ideas can be nurtured into existence. As Shakespeare observed, ideas need names and a 'local habitation'. A look and feel, an elevator description, a key visual in context, all help ideas come to life. Usually it is the ideas with names and contexts that stand out to the creative director, to the client and to the world at large.

Liminal spaces

These are the places in between, where different cultures mix and interact, where personalities shimmer and become more fluid, where hybrid forms are created.

I stole the term liminal spaces from the delightful *Watching the English* (2004) by Kate Fox. (I would suggest that this is essential reading for anyone trying to understand people or consumers or anything at all in England.)

The book unpicks the underlying rules of social grammar that dictate English behaviour, and anyone who lives in England will recognize them instantly when reading it, in particular the 'Importance of *Not Being Earnest*' rule, which helps to explain our pathological reliance on irony.

Fox is an avid people watcher, as social anthropologists tend to be – as advertising people should also be – and she spends a great deal of time in pubs, covertly noting conversations and behaviours.

What she discovers is that pubs are liminal spaces – places where the boundaries blur and normal social rules are overturned. So at the bar you can talk to a random stranger without seeming strange by doing so. People interact. You don't have to be drunk to do so, although we do use alcohol to facilitate this process. There is a communal sense of well-being and a breaking down of barriers that typifies a liminal space.

And then I started thinking, why aren't brand experiences like that? I've been to more than I can remember and people tend to co-exist – not interact – at these things as there is no central, collective experience.

But if a brand could curate a social experience in a liminal space, that was somehow more than a show or a festival, that was an immersive, collective transgression of the normal rules of social behaviour, wouldn't that be an incredibly powerful driver?

Couldn't the right experience help to turn customers into fans? Indeed, in the broadest sense, isn't that the only thing that ever can?

Brainstorms as liminal spaces

Equally, the role of the brainstorm facilitator is to create a liminal space, to bring together different points of view, different ideas, and help them to blend together in a structured, guided way.

The idea and term *brainstorming* was popularized by Alex Osborn (the O in global agency network BBDO) in the 1950s and it has become a staple tool of all creative industries. However, it is often done without preparation and structure, with poor, if any, facilitation, which leads to lacklustre results, groupthink, and wasted time and emotion. This led to a backlash of sorts, championed by Jonah Lehrer in *Imagine: How Creativity Works*, that brainstorming doesn't work.

Having scripted and facilitated hundreds of workshops, I disagree. A well-planned workshop, with the relevant inputs, works excellently for certain things.

One of those things is getting to the interesting parts of the adjacent possible, as fast as possible. Getting the right mix of components and people involved from the start. Blowing through all the most obvious ideas first in order to save the team time.

This is why volume – quantities of concepts – is an important objective. The most compelling are then refined and developed in a more linear way. The facilitator must spend time in advance working through stages 1–3 of the creative process (as set out in the toolkit box above: 'How to have ideas: a genius steals'), and the workshop helps with stages 4 and 5.

Part of stage 6, judgement, can be done in stages: a simple vote in the room, and then more creative direction and refinement following, with pieces of ideas aggregated into larger concepts as appropriate. Of the 100 ideas generated, only 5–10 concepts should emerge.

People often say there are no bad ideas in brainstorms. This is obviously not true; there are many, many bad ideas in brainstorms. And perhaps that's the point.

Creative tenacity

I once saw Adam Morgan, champion of challenger brands, and author of *Eating the Big Fish* (1999) and *The Pirate Inside* (2004) give a talk on a boat on the River Thames. It was very good – a case study in how to use illustrative anecdotes to communicate your points, but there was one bit I particularly latched on to: a concept he called *creative tenacity*.

It means finding a better way of getting through to someone or to an organization – if someone doesn't get your point, find a better way to communicate it. If someone slams the door in your face, don't keep banging on it – find the window.

When he said it, I thought he meant having the tenacity to push through good creative ideas, which isn't what he meant – creative tenacity is a noun phrase in this context (be creative about your tenaciousness). But because I work in the communications industry my brain parsed it incorrectly – creative has a slightly different, and in fact, narrower meaning than it used to have. Within this context it means the people in the creative department, and the work they produce.

It reminds you not to get frustrated when a client/anyone doesn't get you straight away. He used a wonderful example – sadly I forget who it was attributed to:

When I hear no, I take it as request for more information.

It also reminded me of how much what you do channels how you think and how you interpret what you hear. Speaking of which...

The planning paradox

The account planner is often billed as 'the voice of the consumer' within an advertising agency – that ever-elusive man or woman on the omnibus. But when I walk down one of the tunnels in a Tube station, my head swings back and forth looking from ad to ad, to see what's out there, to see if I can work out the thinking behind them.

When I read a newspaper, I look at the ads. When I read a magazine, I look at the ads. When I see an interactive ad in an iPad app, I even sometimes click on it, to see what it does.

Real people don't.

Try it for yourself – next time you are on the Tube, see if anyone even glances at those ads in the tunnels. The only people paying attention, actively, are sure to be advertising practitioners of some kind.

The longer you work as a planner, the longer you work in advertising, the less like an average 'consumer' you are in the way that you attend to advertising, which is probably worth bearing in mind when judging the impact of ideas.

The mediation generation

Virginia Woolf once said that 'nothing has happened until it has been described'.[3] It seems like the rest of the world has caught up with her thought. We endlessly refract ourselves, mediate our lives, to reach out and connect, and then begin to construct ourselves in response to what seems to drive attention our way.

We are making ourselves through mediation.

Online everyone is famous, but some are more famous than others. It's really easy to tell who, because everything is enumerated. As people, we have always thought socially – seeing ourselves through the eyes of others. Increasingly it seems that without mediation, nothing feels real.

The next time you are at a concert – look at all the people capturing the moment on their smartphones, to mediate and broadcast it, to remember it and share it, to continue to create themselves with it – even firsthand experiences require mediation.

The MTV generation was dubbed thus because of the media it *consumed*. The Myspace Generation (now Facebook and Twitter) is perhaps better understood as *The Mediation Generation* because of its tendency to endlessly mediate itself, because of the media it *produces*. As a character from Dave Eggers's novel *The Circle* puts it: 'You and your ilk will live, willingly, joyfully, under constant surveillance, watching each other always, commenting on each other, voting and liking and disliking each other, smiling and frowning, and otherwise doing nothing much else.'

The French philosopher Jean Baudrillard suggested that endless mechanical reproductions of everything make it impossible to tell fantasy from reality – the copies become reality. He called this hyperreality, a kind of reality by proxy, and he said that we had already created a world of simulated stimuli. Umberto Eco called the same idea 'the authentic fake'.

This idea is explored in Charlie Kaufman's film *Synecdoche, New York* (2008), where the director creates and re-creates his own reality in an attempt to understand it and himself. Understanding that the web is public and permanent is embedded in this mediation generation but culturally, rather than individually, we seem to be hurtling into hyper(linked) reality.

We Live in Public is a documentary film that looks at this culture through the lens of a single man's experiments in endless exposure. Josh Harris made millions in the first dot-com boom and ploughed the money into projects designed to foreshadow the world he predicted would be created by the web.

First he set up Pseudo – a web-based television network, in the days of dial-up – then later he built a bunker-like hotel commune called Quiet, where people were filmed 24 hours per day, in every room and activity, and populated it with various art installations and some very strange people (think proto *Big Brother* via a psychedelic lens).

After that he and his girlfriend wired their apartment with sensor-enabled motorized cameras that filmed their every move and streamed it on WeLiveinPublic.com. What he was trying to experiment with, portray, pioneer, sell, was his vision of how the web would change the world, which was that everyone would be watching everyone else, all the time – a polypanopticon.

Perhaps only in our media reflections do we get to see ourselves as we want to be, or perhaps as we want others to see us, which, as in both films, will probably have some very odd effects on our sense of identity at some point – the attention becomes both addictive and a burden.

Eventually, Josh Harris experienced a breakdown that he attributed to his 'media addiction' – consuming and producing himself as an endless feed. He abandoned the web and moved to Ethiopia, a self-imposed rehab – media cold turkey.

We are re-creating our culture as an infinity mirror – a *mise en abyme*, recursive reproductions becoming reality. This means we should probably keep an eye out for signs of cultural breakdown. Fortunately, this shouldn't be too hard since we will be watching ourselves watching each other watching ourselves.

Post-postmodern advertising

The idea that culture is an endless reiteration of old sources is not new (that wouldn't make any sense): 'Most people are other people. Their thoughts are someone else's opinions, their lives a mimicry, their passions a quotation', wrote Oscar Wilde.[4]

But postmodern expression is also characterized by an ironic self-awareness and use of representation – a kind of nudge and a wink to the reader or viewer – that expresses the elusiveness of true meanings.

I think advertising moved into a postmodern mode a long time ago. It has become more and more self-conscious in its self-consciousness for the same reasons that brought about postmodernism in the first place: uncertainty, a lack of absolutes, a feeling that progress is unlikely. The abandonment of anxiety about appropriation could almost be seen as an 'end of (advertising) times' expression.

Every moment in history tends to feel transitional. It seems to be a natural human tendency to feel like Janus, looking backwards at the past and forwards into the future at the same time, applying an ongoing narrative progression to history and, by inference, putting ourselves at an inflection point, at the death and birth of paradigms.

Which is why I'm always a little sceptical of my own tendency to believe that things are changing for the awesome. But my optimism (or possibly meliorism) should and does overcome my scepticism.

The rules that advertising formalized since its inception are slowly breaking down and the modernist certainty of beneficent progress has given way to an industry typified by questions about our validity. This manifests in ads that are either ashamed to be ads (see: any *beautiful piece of film* ad or any piece of branded content) or ads that overcome their shame by being grossly self-aware (see: the bizarre Barry Scott shouting about Cillit Bang).

So what happens next? According to Alan Kirby:

> Postmodernism, like modernism and romanticism before it, fetishised [ie placed supreme importance on] the author, [Note: we may read *author* as *brand*] even when the author chose to indict or pretended to abolish him or herself. But the culture we have now fetishises the recipient of the text to the degree that they become a partial or whole author of it.[5]

This makes sense of the prevailing trend towards the consumer 'being in control' of communication. In postmodern communication the brand reappropriates signs but still remains the central control and focus of the text. Whereas in post-postmodern communication – or *pseudo-modern* – the consumer is an integral part of the creation of the text:

> Its successor, which I will call pseudo-modernism, makes the individual's action the necessary condition of the cultural product. Pseudo-modernism includes all television or radio programmes or parts of programmes, all 'texts', whose content and dynamics are invented or directed by the participating viewer or listener.[6]

The shift to this pseudo-modern mode of communication has been facilitated by emerging communication technologies that allows for traditional media to become interactive. Thus its ultimate expression is online:

> The pseudo-modern cultural phenomenon par excellence is the internet. Its central act is that of the individual clicking on his/her mouse to move through pages in a way which cannot be duplicated, inventing a

pathway through cultural products which has never existed before and never will again.[7]

This is why pseudo-modern communications tend to lean towards co-creation, interaction, engagement – consumers are integral to the construction of the texts – and this reaches far beyond the sudden explosion of *user-generated content* advertising campaigns.

For example, Google leveraged consumer input online before deciding on their very first television advertisement. It almost always makes sense to launch any film online before it hits television, but then the two work powerfully together. This is because the online audience is still interested in discovery and primacy. In order to share something, you have to have the sense that it hasn't already been seen by everyone. The TV audience, however, doesn't really care if a film has been online already, because the internet is an infinite space, and the modality of consumption is different.

Google ran their first-ever TV spot 'Parisian Love' during Super Bowl 2010, having first conceived of it as an 'online film' according to CEO Eric Schmidt,[8] which they ran alongside others to see which earned the greatest number of views, before making the winner a Super Bowl spot.

It has since become *de rigueur* to launch your Super Bowl spot online first. Volkswagen's 'The Force' spot,[9] featuring a child dressed as Darth Vader, hijacked the conversation around advertising in Super Bowl 2011, because it was launched weeks in advance.

In 2013, Coca-Cola more fully adopted a pseudo-modern mode, launching their Super Bowl spot even earlier, and inviting the audience to decide what happens. The 60-second 'Mirage' features three teams racing across the desert towards a giant Coca-Cola bottle, which as the title suggests, is a mirage. The viewer is then given control of the resolution. They were directed to CokeChase.com, where they could vote on which will 'win' the Coca-Cola.

We can offer people the sense that they are in control of their interaction with the brand and that their interaction, their attention, is a requisite condition for its existence.

Because, ultimately, they are and it is.

TOOLKIT Combination tool for brand behaviour

Let's look back at the elements of the brand behaviour model.

The brand belief is the guiding principle, the belief about the world that needs to be expressed by ideas. The elements of the model are components:

- product;

- service;

- action;

- content;

- tool;

- advertising.

A simple combination tool to open up new idea areas is to combine these in different ways. Each combination creates a new idea area:

- Content + tool = content tool (ie that could be tools that help consumers to create content).

- Advertising + tool = advertising tool (ie that could be tools to interact with the advertising, like the Coca-Cola example above).

- Action + content = action content (ie content that is reportage of a brand action).

- Product + service = product service (ie create a service extension of the product, or a product extension of the service).

And recombine them:

- Content tool + advertising = ad campaign generated by consumers using a content tool.

- Product service + content = content that demonstrates the service extension, or shows people using it.

And so on. Combinatorics (the maths of combinations) shows that there are 63 possible combinations, or areas to explore, of these six elements, which should provide plenty of starting points of ideas.

Advertising for advertising

Is the industry paying attention?

What are advertising awards for?

How advertising creates value is complicated.

Business objectives are, for the most part, simple. Businesses like to make, or save, money. Increasing revenue or profit are the key objectives. However, too often in advertising, we displace these objectives with intermediate ones, ones that come *on the way* to money, ones whose measurement we can control such as prompted awareness, or purchase intent, as measured by surveys. If it doesn't make, or save, money it is not a business objective, since that is what businesses want to achieve. (There are some exceptions, such as recruitment advertising, but for the most part, it is about money.)

Anything else is an *intermediate* measure, based on an assumed model of how some kind of process works: like if more people e-mail me maybe I will sell them more stuff, or if loads of people like the films we put on in between television programmes maybe they will buy more of my stuff later. Or if people have paid attention to my brand, maybe they will pay more money for it. But don't forget this is a model and, as we know, all are wrong but some are useful.

Ultimately, it depends on what you believe changes behaviour, and how you then decide to measure that. The simplest ROI model

– looking at the cost of production, media and fees for an advertising campaign for a consumer-packaged good (CPG) product and then measuring the incremental sales attributable to that campaign, assuming a decay rate of the impact over time after broadcast, using multivariate regression analysis to untangle the effect of the advertising – is actually far from simple.

It also tends not to show positive results in a lot of cases, especially with mature brands that have all the background awareness they could possibly need, if not all the attention. But then you get things like intangible asset value and goodwill, which also have commercial value on balance sheets when sold, and price elasticity of demand, both of which seem to be sensitive to communications.

This is why I usually laugh when someone says: 'Digital is unproven, but we can show that TV works!'

Seven habits of highly effective communication

In an industry where accolades are mostly bestowed by peer review and creative judgement, we leave ourselves open to the charge that we forget what we are here for, which is, usually, to help clients make money.

Give thanks, then, for the Effie awards (Effies), which honour the effectiveness of the work we do in creating value for clients. I mean value here very specifically, in the sense of dollars and cents required to get it out the door and that shows, overall, that the investment (in money and time and sweat and tears... but mostly the money) were recouped and returned upon with interest.

In 2012 I was an Effies judge and for the first time they issued a report with detailed analysis that unpicks some of the drivers of efficacy among the finalists that year. What differentiates those that won a medal from those that were pipped at the post? All the short-listed have demonstrated efficacy to some level, so what separates the great from the good?

TOOLKIT   Seven habits of highly effective communication: what separates the great from the good at the Effie awards?

1. Start with business objectives

Effectiveness is the capability of producing a desired result. Since we are looking to make clients money, it makes sense to start with those objectives and then parse them into marketing. Keeping financial and your own innovative KPIs in mind seems to work. (Remember to establish SMART objectives: specific, measurable, attainable, relevant, time bound.)

2. Do some interesting, useful research

As already discussed, I have a number of epistemological issues with how much market research is done, but that doesn't mean I don't believe in research. It is crucial that we base our solutions to problems on cogent data, as we attempt to craft symbols and actions to solve problems.

The Silver Effie awarded to Febreze/Ambi Pur for the 'Breathe Happy' campaign makes this case well.[1] The highly immersive research included various kinds of olfactory research, deprivation experiments, in-home ethnographic elements and assisted shopping. The research led directly to the creative idea, where consumers are blindfolded, put into rooms full of foul-smelling stuff, sprayed with Febreze and asked to describe the odours they encounter.

3. Believe in strategy

Despite certain vocal members of the industry declaiming the death of strategy, the analysis is very clear: 'The most salient characteristic defining gold... was the quality of the strategy.'[2]

So don't listen to people who say it is dead. (Indeed, anyone using the 'death of' narrative should be considered with caution.) Strategy crafts business solutions, leveraging compelling insight into behaviour and cultural context, informing the need for and role of advertising. As we shall see in Chapter 10, strategy is evolving to serve the new context.

4. 'Boldness has genius, power and magic in it' (Goethe)

Small, scrappy companies facing off against giant corporations is a story that plays out again and again, appearing often as Effie award winners. We all love an underdog, but perhaps more importantly we should understand that audacious goals – moonshots, to use a Google term – are galvanizing. Rarely do brands have opinions, but when they do they are rewarded with attention. Take a stand, pick a side, even when your consumers might not *all* share the same opinion. When Oreo posted their rainbow Oreo in support of gay pride, they doubled their daily fan growth.[3]

5. Integration as the interoperation of parts, not one idea in many places

The analysis makes the distinction between 'woven' and just 'layered' media. We are increasingly in the age of systems and the interoperation of parts to create a larger whole, rather than media that is 'added together'.

6. Do it, ideally with the community, don't just say it

As Millward Brown states: 'The era of claim-based advertising, while not entirely gone, is certainly not winning Effie awards.'[4] The much-vaunted era of engagement is upon us, but brands have to earn that engagement.

The 'Curators of Sweden' project has won awards across shows and categories. What better way to communicate how socially liberal and fundamentally democratic Sweden is, around the world, for almost no money, than to give the country's Twitter account over to a different one of its citizens every week, with no censorship as to what they say, even when one of the participants posted this: 'Once my 4-year old found Marijuana and porn in my bicycle-wagon. I keep that wagon in our basement. That was a little odd wasn't it?'

7. Unleash creativity through constraint

The Effies, above all, value creativity in service of the goal. Winning entries have highly focused problems that are being demonstrably solved. This is where the business needs are alchemically transmuted into an understanding of human behaviour.

This is where non-obvious connection is filtered through craft into the world – and changes something. And make sure that you establish that this solution – be it advertising or shopper marketing – is the optimal one for the problem at hand.

Awarding creativity

As already suggested, creative awards are something of a double-edged sword.

On the one hand, they are the highest accolades we bestow on our ourselves for what we do. We are rightly proud to give (and accept) them, as tokens of both recognition for great work done, and indication of the kind of work we hope the industry will do in the future.

On the other hand, since they are awarded based solely on creative judgement, they leave us open to the ever-present attack that we forget what we are here to do, which is to create business results for our clients, to provide returns on marketing investment.

Fortunately, Donald Gunn's eponymous report (written with Emma Wilkie), which tallies across many of the global creative awards shows, has been fused with the IPA databank, which holds the results of the IPA Effectiveness awards. The research shows, among other things, that ads that win creative awards are 11 times more efficient at delivering business success than those that don't.[5]

So rejoice in the awards! For the best, most awarded work, works best.

Additionally, agencies are often criticized for focusing on awards as it distracts them from their primary business of servicing clients. Awards are a point of pride for agencies, a way of packaging and merchandising their work for posterity and, importantly, they provide a metric of reputation. Thus, agencies that win more awards attract better talent. In fact, creative director Simon Veksner once suggested that awards per head is how creatives should pick agencies to work for:

> Let's assume you are lucky enough to be offered more than one job. How do you know which agency is better?
>
> Well, there are lots of factors that will be particular to you – whether you like the people, the agency's style of work, and its location, for example. But the most important factor, by far, is Awards Per Head.
>
> For reasons we all understand, and have discussed many times before, nothing will help your career more than awards. Therefore, the best agency is the agency that wins the most awards per creative team.[6]

Since individuals want to win awards to help their own careers, as in every industry, agencies that neglect them can suffer. But perhaps most importantly, whilst it is often claimed that clients don't care about awards, I have never encountered any who didn't like them. In fact, awards help to attract attention to ideas and agencies – they function *as advertising for advertising*. So suggesting that awards distract agencies from their core business is analogous to saying that advertising is a distraction for companies since they make and sell widgets.

Trial by jury

I have been fortunate to sit on innumerable advertising creative award juries, including the Campaign awards, the Art Director's Club awards, The One Show and numerous others. I have also been privileged to chair several of them, including the Content&Contact Jury and the Integrated Jury for the Clio awards. I helped to create an entirely new category for the London International awards, called 'The NEW Category', to highlight new *kinds* of advertising.[7] This is what I wrote in my judge's comments about our hope for the NEW:

> The need was obvious – there was so much great work that just didn't fit anywhere else. It needed a category that could recognize it.
>
> It's always worth keeping an eye on things that don't fit in elsewhere as mutations are the key to evolution. It was very much with this in mind that we approached the judging. We wanted to make sure the winners pointed in fruitful possible directions; that the ideas increased the vocabulary of the industry.
>
> We looked for ideas that created new engagement spaces between people and companies, or that hacked existing ones; things that consumers latched on to and spread; marketing that was of such value that people were willing to pay to consume it (but aren't they called products? Maybe. Perhaps the distinction is getting blurry); and ideas that pulled new technologies into the useful service of brands and their customers.[8]

Working with agencies, helping them put award entries together, demonstrated to me how invaluable the experience of judging is when it comes to crafting entries.

Studying cases

In the standard categories, the work is defined by medium: film, radio, outdoor and so on; but in the new categories, such definitions don't work because the new ideas do not sit inside boxes of the past. If an idea is a system of participation, the craft elements itself are not enough to judge the idea. Without the audience doing something, the ideas don't work.

Thus, in the early years of the noughties, the case-study video emerged as a way to package up the system and enter the newer categories for award shows. The case study is advertising for advertising, which indicates how they should be made.

TOOLKIT   How to create a case study

A good case study tends to have:

- *An objective, a problem to solve*: because we are in the business of solving problems with creativity.

- *Some sense of the audience and context*: because ideas that make no sense to an American juror, for example, could be breakthrough pieces of culture in, say, Japan.

- *Insight*: something gleaned or uncovered that led to the solution.

- *Solution*: the strategic idea that leads to creative solution.

- *Execution*: the work itself, or people engaging with it.

- *Impact*: not just whatever numbers you can muster, but something that indicates the impact the idea had on culture and business (ie not only impressions).

- *Story and understanding*: humour, surprise, empathy, and understanding the audience (which for a case study in an award show is other advertising folk, sitting for 10 hours a day in a dark room, watching hundreds of videos) are all excellent elements to making better case studies, as they are with advertisements.

Some senior creative directors now much malign the case study as distracting the industry from the work itself, from the craft. The case study has become an artefact in its own right and there are problems with this, especially when their veracity is not rigorously checked, but getting rid of them seems impossible in an age when the nature of the work we do continues to change. We cannot simply *show the work*, if the work is an experience, or a piece of software that must be used, or a participatory programme.

To complain about the distraction of making case studies seems to me to be, again, analogous to complaining that a company wastes time making ads, since it distracts from their core business. Unless, of course, they mean we should be outsourcing the case studies to other companies, as companies do with their advertising.

Integrative strategy and social brands
Be nice or leave!

We tend to overestimate the effect of technology in the short run and underestimate the effect in the long run. AMARA'S LAW

The emergence of a strategist at an agency characterizes a moment of tension, a grinding caused by the varying rates of change inside and outside the organization. A strategist must be able to recommend the solution that has the best chance of solving the problem. Strategy allocates investment as well as insight. Whilst many agency planning heads transmogrified into chief strategy officers, this title change is only necessary, surely, if it means something different than that which came before. Strategy, as we shall see, informs the need for advertising, whereas account planning informs the advertising. This sets up a strategy function in opposition to the rest of the agency, if the agency is predominantly allied to a set spectrum of executions, since strategy must be able to recommend something else.

Even allowing the domain of the agency strategist to be communications, this still requires considering the ever-increasing set of options and tackling deeply embedded assumptions about what agencies do. The emergence of integration as a problem for clients and a management function across clients and agencies is a symptom of this problem. Integration suggests putting the disparate together. What we need now is *integrative strategy* that starts holistically and selects the best solution set from the range of options, rather than trying to put the same thing in every possible place. The ultimate question becomes: is advertising, as we currently understand it, still the best way to capture attention? The answer, unfortunately, is not 42.[1]

What do advertising agencies actually do?

Outside the industry, it is little recognized that advertising agencies do not actually make television commercials – this is outsourced to production companies. Advertising agencies germinate, direct and manage the processes of advertising production. However, the question is more fundamental than this – what are advertising agencies for?

In 1960 Harvard professor Theodore Levitt wrote his classic paper 'Marketing Myopia'. Levitt points out that every industry was once a growth industry but that never lasts, not because the market is saturated, but rather because companies misinterpret the fundamental question 'What business are you in?'

One of his key examples is the US railroads. Once a mighty growth industry, it declined steeply because it failed to recognize the threat presented by the emergence and eventual affordability of cars and trips inside the '100 ton tubes of metal moving smoothly through the air 20,000 feet above the earth, loaded with 100 sane and solid citizens casually drinking martinis'.[2] The railroad tycoons thought they were in the business of railroads when they were really in the business of transport – they were myopically *product focused* instead of being *customer focused*. This idea has become an adage of marketing, aphoristically captured by Levitt himself:

> People don't want to buy a quarter-inch drill. They want a quarter-inch hole![3]

It is the same logic that might have prevented Kodak from its ignominious fall from grace – Kodak was not in the 'film' business that digital cameras abruptly destroyed, it was in the business of capturing memories – it just didn't adapt until much too late. This is an example of the *innovator's dilemma,* as coined by Clayton Christensen. Kodak was the first to develop digital cameras but shelved the technology in order to avoid cannibalizing its core business and confusing its existing customers. This in turn left it open to be decimated by new entrants when the market changed.

Advertising agencies 'make' advertisements and this is a surprisingly healthy business considering how often its demise has been trumpeted. Indeed, television advertising in the United States grew a healthy 9.7 per cent in 2010 after the nadir of the recession,[4] and growth is projected to continue. Despite ad-skipping digital video recorders, the death of the 30-second spot has been greatly exaggerated.

That said, it is important to remember that advertising is a drill, not a hole.

Advertising is a means, not an end, a lever designed to affect consumer behaviour leading people to pay price premiums and buy more things, more often, due to the dimly understood interactions of persuasive symbols and human cognitive, social and economic behaviour.

Thus, should better, more efficient, more effective solutions to the business problem of marketing products to the masses manifest, companies would be well advised to pursue them. Advertising agencies, then, either 'make' advertising, which is a service that can be displaced, or they help corporations to solve business problems with creativity, which will remain an ongoing need as long as there are corporations – but puts 'advertising' agencies into a much larger competitive set alongside other business consultants, albeit with a specific competitive advantage. Agencies are able to effectively house and manage commercially creative people, which management consultancies struggle with for the same reason that corporations do – the environment is not very palatable to them.

The business of advertising remains robust for now but the business of ideas that drive business growth is evergreen. The industry is bifurcating along these lines.

It is a good idea to work out which business you want to be in and act accordingly. Pure play advertising agencies should leverage their core competencies inside the extant market. Agencies that want to explore the possibilities outside this definition must be willing to invest in developing new competencies to service emerging needs, increasingly at the intersection of technology and storytelling. This blurriness is perhaps best evinced by the ONE CLUB awarding Nike+ as the 'digital campaign of the decade' despite or, because of, the fact that it is not a campaign. A technology-driven product/service extension attracts and earns attention for a brand, solving a problem with something other than 'advertising'. The Nike+ FuelBand was similarly a powerful brand idea for Nike, positioning them at the forefront of the wearable technology and quantified self trends, but not a successful product – it was discontinued in 2014.

Both routes are sensible to consider, depending on an honest analysis of the business and its strengths, including its key and often over-looked intangible asset, the agency brand. The danger comes from attempting to be all things to all customers, the chimera of the 'full service agency'.

The essence of strategy is trade-offs, since finite resources necessitate finite offerings. Worse than not making decisions is falling victim to the *Shirky principle* – an idea established by Clay Shirky in his book *Cognitive Surplus* (2010) and elevated to the status of principle by Kevin Kelly, founding editor of *Wired*. Shirky explains that:

> Institutions will try to preserve the problem to which they are the solution.[5]

Rather than solving clients problems, then, agencies that succumb to the principle spend their energies trying to maintain that the world of business and media hasn't changed, or attempting to stymie symptoms of the change when they encounter it.

As with any corporate strategy, the road ahead for advertising depends on knowing what business you are really in and acting accordingly.

What strategy is and is not

The word strategy comes from the Greek *strategos*, which translates roughly as general, and then came to mean the art of the general. This is why MBA types often read *The Art of War* (1913) by Sun Tzu. Or at least pretend to.

Strategy, as an idea, is simple. You have a goal you wish to achieve. You have finite resources that can be deployed in achieving it. Strategy is simply *how*.

In my early professional life I was a management consultant. Whilst I wasn't a huge fan of the dress code, I did like the grounding it gave me in strategy. I became very familiar with the BCG matrix,[6] Porter's five forces model,[7] and the tenets of business as espoused by Harvard Business School.

And, again, it's simple. Remember, businesses exist solely to create value, to make money. Therefore, business strategy is simply how you intend to go about doing that, using whatever assets you have available. Everything else, brand strategy (how to leverage the intangible asset that is brand) and creative strategy (what the proposition is that informs the advertising), exist only in service of that.

But creative strategy concerns itself with the content, tone and messaging of advertising, which may not be necessarily useful for creating ideas that are something else. This has led some smart people to suggest that planners need to get their hands dirty and start making things, diving into a world of prototyping. No doubt there is value in the act of making, but not every idea can be prototyped.

And if planners start making things, would they still be planners? A friend of mine once said: 'Surely the only thing a planner should make, by definition, is a plan.'

Planning for the future

Account planning is a young discipline and has reached a moment of inflection. Historically, account planning played a number of roles within an advertising agency. It is the discipline that, through research and insight, brings the voice of the consumer into the process of developing advertising. The planner directs and inspires the creative work so that it is more likely to achieve the desired business result. The role was created to provide the process of advertising development with a more scientific foundation. Now, the proliferation of marketing disciplines, changes to the consumer and media environment, and our understanding of human behaviour are all changing the parameters of the role, and indeed how we must think about advertising in general.

The increasing complexity of the communication landscape has led to a fragmentation of strategy across disciplines and departments, which requires an expansion, at the very least, of traditional planning: 'There definitely is a problem where you have a multi-agency structure team where there are planners in each of the respective disciplines.'[8]

Recent developments in behavioural economics and psychology suggest that models we have historically used to understand how advertising works are wrong, or at least not the whole story. Advertising as 'salesmanship in print' and 'message transmission' are both being fundamentally challenged.[9]

As we explored in the first half of the book, research suggests that consciously held attitudes do not necessarily change behaviour, despite the counter-intuitive experience of conscious will,[10] but that feelings, relationships and associations are more important behavioural drivers, which are less influenced by messaging and more by 'metacommunication',[11] and that heuristics and biases are equally important, which mostly operate outside our own conscious experience of them.

Social copying is often the driver for truly successful marketing, since it spreads beyond the initial receiving audience. (Remember our discussions of viral and what it isn't?) Once in a while, advertising transcends the stratum reserved for commercial communication and becomes a cultural phenomenon – quite literally something that can be seen to have an effect on culture.

My old colleague Yusuf Chuku, now head of strategy for McKinney NYC, upon reading my previous thoughts about the 118-118 directory-enquiries T-shirts launch campaign (discussed in Chapter 3), pointed out that the truly viral part of the campaign, which ascended into the collective consciousness, was shouting 'Got your number!' at people in the street. They did it in the ads,[12] then the boys hit the streets and did it 'in real life'. Then everyone was doing it – it echoed across popular culture and into the parlance. Just as it did for Pears soap all those years ago.

The ultimate aim of all commercial communication is to spread ideas that elicit a behavioural response. Specifically, we usually want to influence mass purchase behaviour. But if a brand can propagate some intermediate behaviours, like getting people to shout 'Got your number' or 'Wassup!'[13] (as Budweiser did) at each other, then you get some additional benefits.

Before consumer-generated content was a *thing*, people made and shared hundreds of 'Wassup' spoofs,[14] spreading the brand idea much further than the original did. The behaviour recalls and reinforces the brand, keeping the brand salient. And, behaviour is transmissible. Humans are hardwired to learn by imitating. The drive to copy is so powerful that, for example, when children are shown behaviours they know are pointless to achieve required goals in a test, they imitate them anyway.[15]

Monkey see, monkey do. Except actually, monkeys and primates don't – only people do. In extreme cases, when this behavioural imitation becomes pathological, it is called echopraxia. We are built to copy behaviour.

CASE STUDY

Behavioural engineering of this type was at the heart of many of BBH's successful ideas for the deodorant Lynx/Axe. Young males are particularly prone to adopting learned behaviours. Many Lynx ideas have imitative behaviours at their core. For the launch of Lynx Pulse the agency invented a dance. They found a track – a remix of a minor hit, 'Get Down Saturday Night' by Oliver Cheatham, called 'Make Luv' – and worked with a choreographer to create a dance, one that turns a geeky guy into a bar star. As John O'Keefe, executive creative director (ECD) at BBH at the time, said: 'To be easy to copy, a dance has to be modular. What proved particularly effective was that while it was copy-able, it took numerous viewings of the... ad for the viewer to pick up all the modules. Our target audience simply had to watch it again and again and again.'[16] The dance was seeded by brand ambassadors at student events all over Britain before the ad launched so that the dance seemed to have emerged into culture organically. When it did finally launch, the dance became a craze, the single went straight to number one, and Lynx Pulse became the biggest-selling brand variant within two weeks. The Lynx Click variant was launched on television with an advertisement featuring Ben Affleck using a tally counter to count the number of women who 'check him out'. This behaviour was seeded prior to broadcast in Australia by sponsoring an unbranded tour for a local hip-hop duo, Weapon X and Hell, who demonstrated the behaviour that was being branded and distributed tally counters. 'Bom Chicka Wah Wah' was a made-up expression, uttered in the presence of arousing people or situations. All designed to create influence through imitation.

If you want to influence behaviour, give people something to copy.

Many of these ideas about behaviour being directed by sub-conscious drivers contradict our internal perceptions of choice and action, leading to persistent meta-cognitive errors in how we approach advertising. We think we think how we think, as it were. They lay bare the problems of market research that attempts to unpick unconscious drivers solely by interrogating the conscious mind.

The socialization of media

'Social media' – which is created by the many, rather than the few – have been a long time coming. Henry Jenkins established the blurring of media modalities in 2006 in his prescient book about the participatory nature of digital media, *Convergence Culture* – in a digital world of democratized creative tools and access, everyone who consumes can create, everyone who receives can broadcast.

But it wasn't until 'creation' was whittled down to 140 characters and clipped fragments of the web, as with Twitter and Tumblr, that it became obvious that since everyone was talking and sharing, people were expecting content to move in concert.

In January 2011, Twitter's new CEO crystallized the company's vision: 'We want to instantly connect people everywhere to what's most important to them.'[17]

One of the key tenets of a *media system* approach is that every new channel changes the entire system. So, because YouTube exists, how we think about 'television' has to change. Regardless of whether or not your idea or marketing campaign has a digital component – the world does.

Be nice or leave

All media are social.

<RANT>We should remember that media is the nominative plural of the word medium. It is especially important to remember this to avoid using the world *mediums* to refer to multiple media, which seems almost endemic now, but is still wrong. Language evolves, of course, but that word already has another meaning. So, unless many people in advertising are talking about a group of people who claim to be able to channel the dead, it's wrong.</RANT>

Let's start with the problem of naming things. We used to call 'it' Web 2.0, before that consumer-generated content. Now we call 'it' social media. This is still problematic.

When we use the word 'media' in the advertising industry it has a diminished meaning that triggers a certain set of associations and behaviours. Due to the way we understand 'media agencies', when we hear the word media, we often begin to unconsciously think of 'something that I can buy space in to put ads', which is not the best way to think of social media. This is what led to the adoption of a broader media model by said agencies, combining Paid, Owned and Earned Media (POEM).[18]

Emerging cultural practices

When looking at this emerging mediascape, the tendency is to simply catalogue platforms. This approach is not entirely helpful. Whilst understanding Facebook or Twitter is important, technologies are superseded: Friendster begat Myspace begat Facebook. As Henry Jenkins has pointed out: 'Our focus should not be on emerging technologies but on emerging cultural practices.'[19]

Social media are centred on two cultural practices: conversations and relationships – people talking to each other, one to one and one to many, and establishing and reinforcing different kinds of relationships. These two practices are two sides of the same coin.

In anthropology there is a concept known as *phatic* communication, which is highly relevant to social spaces. Advertising is, for the most part, paradigmatically wed to the idea that communication is about the transmission of messages. However, the vast majority of communication transmits little semantically: the dominant function of the interaction is phatic – it is designed to establish and re-enforce relationships. Status updates do not transmit crucial data – they just keep the relationship alive, a ping making sure that the network is still there. *I exist, I'm okay. You exist, you're okay. The network is open and flowing.* This is the substructure of phatic interactions, according to anthropologist Grant McCracken.[20] Facebook's poke function was the ultimate phatic communication tool, where any shred of message is stripped out from the medium.

Social graces

Brands need to consider the social media ecosystem. People are more likely to believe a random blog post than a television commercial due to the erosion of trust (as discussed in Chapter 3, with specific reference to Nielsen's Global Trust in Advertising Survey). As consumers spend more time consuming each other's content, mainstream media's share of attention will continue to erode. Brands need to find a way to be relevant in these new spaces.

Fortunately, understanding how to behave in social media is easy. You already know the answer because you are a social creature and because you read the subtitle of the chapter: *be nice or leave!*

This is not to sound trite – being nice is an entirely different behavioural grammar for marketers. There are two overlapping types of grammar that dictate human behaviour. We have already challenged the myth of *homo economicus* – a rational being responds to a money incentive with an increased propensity to perform an action. Social grammar is a different incentive framework.

An interesting feature of the two modes of behaviour, pointed out by behavioural economist Dan Ariely in *Predictably Irrational*, is that they don't mix. Acting commercially in social spaces can be insulting and inappropriate, which is perhaps why corporations, commercial entities with commercial motivations, find it difficult to act socially.

You can easily test for yourself how poorly they mix: the next time that someone you love cooks you a meal, in order to show appreciation and encourage this behaviour – leave a tip. Despite what classical economics suggests, this is unlikely to encourage the behaviour.

That said, I outline below an approach for brands looking to begin to interact with the social world. First however, two caveats:

- Being social needs dedicated resources – building relationships takes time and constant attention.

- You cannot control what people say. In order to play in social spaces you must trade control for influence – something that many corporations are still uncomfortable with.

TOOLKIT   Six steps to being social

1. Listen

People are talking about every brand. They provide conversational focal points among the loosely connected. Free tools like Google Alerts and Twitter searches show you what they are saying.
Paid services like radian6, Expion, Sysomos offer a larger set of functions. Like any conversation, it begins with listening.

2. Respond

On the internet, conversations *about* you are often directed *to* you. It is expected that you are listening, and should you encounter people reaching out, someone should be responding to complaints and questions: 70 per cent of brands still ignore customer complaints on Twitter,[21] which, by this stage, seems rude.

3. Nurture

The first corporate response to social media was: get me one. Wal-Mart attempted to build its own social network. This didn't work because there was no social object tying the network together, no reason for it to exist. As Mark Zuckerberg has pointed out: 'You don't start communities. Communities already exist... think about how you can help that community do what it wants to do.'[22]

   If people are already out there discussing your brand, nurture them.

4. Create social objects

'The key is to produce something that both pulls people together and gives them something to do'

HENRY JENKINS[23]

People like to socialize and they like to do things together – the highest hope for a social marketing effort is that it becomes a social object itself. When launching the Nikon D40, the agency gave 200 cameras to a small town – *PictureTown* – and let them find out for themselves how easy they were to use, creating reams of social content in the process.

5. Be transparent

Let's be very clear about this – lying is wrong.

Back in the early days of the social web there was a lot of shady work creating fake grass-roots movements (digital astroturfing, if you will). I had assumed that this was a thing of the past. However, people are always tempted. One particularly silly example came from a marketing manager at Belkin, a company that makes routers, who was caught offering to pay people to write positive reviews of the products on Amazon. This is quite staggeringly foolish. On the social web, when someone knows something, everyone knows something. The fact that he was offering the payment on Mechanical Turk, an online marketplace that is part of Amazon, beggars belief. Pranks, or faked reportage, are also dangerous territory as they can precipitate a backlash. Instead of playing a joke *on* your consumers, let them in on the joke.

6. Join the conversation

This can take innumerable forms. This is when the brand begins the shift from acting like a faceless corporation and makes the transition to an appropriate grammar for the space. It is here that content strategy begins to emerge as a crucial new discipline. Once you have joined the conversation, you will want to go back to listening to understand how people respond. And so, instead of a list, it is really a cycle.

Social communication is fundamentally different. It requires a different behavioural grammar, different skills and different staffing. To finish with a line from Scott Monty, head of social media at Ford: 'it is not about campaigns; it is about commitment'.[24]

Cultural latency

There is more to life than increasing its speed.

GANDHI

There is a correlation between the amount of time it takes to distribute something, and the amount of time it takes for that thing to have an effect, and consequently the amount of time that thing stays relevant and interesting.

When music was distributed as sheet music – a (literally) laborious distribution mechanism, since you had to learn how to play and then perform – popular hits stayed at the top of the charts for years. When gramophone reproductions were introduced, the half-life of a hit decreased dramatically.

You don't need to learn to play piano to use a disc, so this removes a distribution bottleneck: piano and pianist. The latency decreased again each time formats became easier to distribute, for either technological or structural reasons.

Digital distribution removes many of the friction points within the system, making it more efficient. This also seems to lead to far more rapid cultural decay rates. In gaming, and network-based computing in general, the term that describes the lag between a cause and effect, between the moment when something is initiated and the moment one of the effects can be perceived, is *latency*.

The lower the latency, the faster the distant computer responds, the faster you see an effect and can respond and so on. Low latency is a good thing – it means you don't get killed in the game because your character didn't move when you told it to.

As communication technologies get faster and more pervasive, the latency of culture is decreasing. The speed at which people could move used to be the speed at which information travelled, which is why Pheidippides ran 26 miles to deliver news about the Battle of Marathon. The speed at which messages could traverse distances put a limit on the latency of culture, which in turn tended to mean that things changed more slowly.

E-mail messages travel at almost the speed of light as electrons along copper wire and photons inside optical fibre. This led to things moving faster, things changing faster, but e-mail is point to point – even if you send it to many people, no one oversees the message, which puts a limit on the reduction in cultural latency – and it used to be limited to the desktop.

Now we have millions of high-resolution eyes connected to real-time micro-broadcast messaging platforms via a mobile device and a social eagerness to demonstrate primacy.

Cultural latency seems to be approaching zero, at least in the more connected parts of the world. I suspect this is going to have some interesting effects, because it creates much faster feedback loops. Information, once delivered, is both an effect and a subsequent cause, which triggers more effects, and so on. Things like informational cascades, previously very visible in stock markets (which constantly monitor and report on themselves), and cumulative advantages, which function when behaviour is visible to the decision-making crowd, will inevitably become more prevalent. Things like swine flu or Ebola can go from something no one has heard of, to something people are searching for, to a topic of *twysteria*, literally overnight.

The infosphere is beginning to operate more chaotically: a dynamic, closed, evolving system, characterized by aperiodic feedback loops that can drive massive perturbations in the system from relatively small changes in the initial conditions. Diminished cultural latency means that the propagation of information is so fast that the spread itself becomes the defining aspect of the system: the rate-of-spread becomes as important as the information itself.

The *speed* of medium is the message, perhaps.

Ghostwriting for brands

Ghostwriters make a living taking words from the famous and putting them to paper. And, of course, advertising has long spoken for brands – in a very specific context.

Now, the web allows for, and seems to insist on, direct connections with customers, prospects, fans and detractors. This, in turn, has created a far greater need for content, as distinct from advertising.

Content is something they want to hear; advertising is something we want to say.

The Cannes Lions Advertising Festival announced their newest category – Branded Content – in 2012, to reflect this rapidly growing sector of the industry. Various agencies have created new content units staffed with former journalists to service these needs. Brands of sufficient scale have also begun to create their own newsrooms, staffed with journalists and filmmakers. Nissan was one of the earliest; Oreo, one of the most cited.

People suddenly find themselves ghostwriting for brands in a new way. This is because, on Facebook, brand content co-mingles with consumer-created content, which flows at a very high frequency compared to advertising – Facebook reports that the average user creates 90 pieces of content per month[25] – and rarely repeats itself.

Content strategy, in essence what the editorial function of media has always done, is being developed for brands to maintain these ongoing relationships at the frequency the environment and audience dictates. It is a huge challenge and opportunity for brands and their agents, as they look to develop more depth and complexity to maintain an ongoing content stream. With immediate feedback as to what content resonates with a community comes the opportunity to adapt in real time. Inside the stream we can experiment with much smaller fragments of content that require tiny individual investments, and keep learning as we go.

Created content is supplemented with curated content from across the web, helping brands to turn themselves into signals in the noise, with context or commentary from the brand's point of view appended by a community manager and then fed to the brand's social streams. Software companies such as Percolate help to manage this process,[26] by creating a unique set of sources for each brand, filtering them into daily content recommendations, and managing the process of permissions, creation and social distribution as well.

Content can be as simple as a status update, as complex as a documentary film. Some advertising, made for broadcast, is repurposed as social content. Very occasionally this works, but usually it doesn't because of the difference in how they were conceived: advertising looks to say something a company wants to say in the most appealing way possible to an audience, whereas content starts from thinking about what the audience wants to consume and then considers how the brand can add value to that. They start from opposite ends.

Are you engaged?

Engagement is the thing wherein I'll catch the attention of the consumer!

So goes the current thinking. Forget all that push stuff that we can't break through. There is too much clutter, too many channels, too many brands, and 30-second spots don't work any more anyway. Everyone either gets up for snacks during commercials or screens them out with TiVo. I'll use the Web instead, and then consumers will seek me out and bathe in my brand to their hearts' content.

Well, maybe.

But with hundreds of millions of websites out there and a new blog created every second, the web has become more cluttered and fragmented than any other medium. It is no longer enough for a brand to use digital communications merely as a platform to deliver a message or create an experience. Now smart brands take it a giant step further: 'They strive to make their communication channels provide a service value, too.'[27]

Or so I co-wrote for an article that was published on 1 September 2006 – 25 days before Facebook was opened to people outside of academic institutions with an e-mail address and three months before the iPhone was announced. We were hinting at what became known as 'branded utility' – but could perhaps be put under the bigger umbrella of earning attention – using pieces of brand-created software as the primary examples.

Now, of course, branded apps are commonplaces – but earning attention is increasingly difficult and so we have begun to trade an obsession with awareness for an obsession with engagement. We live in an oft-heralded age of engagement but we should remind ourselves that brands don't want engagement, or awareness, or relationships, except as a means. Neither do their customers.

Engagement simply indicates, perhaps, that those ever-fickle consumers were in fact paying attention to our efforts. On Facebook, brands have to learn how to engage on an ongoing basis, a cadence that is very different to the campaign deployments of old.

Engagement covers a lot of different ideas, but online it is most often measured by looking at not how many people had the opportunity to see the idea, but rather what impact that had on their immediate behaviour (time spent with a site or story or application, comments and approval, retweets and so on), which is a marked improvement – looking at behavioural intermediate effects in a world where every-one can both consume and produce content seems sensible. (If a piece of branded anything falls in the stream and no one tweets about it, did it have any effect?)

Whilst considering how to better engage, despite the fact that con-sumers are inherently participatory online, it is important to remember they also have better things to do than to engage with brands, unless we give them a good reason to do so (or they have unsolved issues, as we have seen). An open letter to advertisers, posted online in 2010, for example, humorously suggested that perhaps the manufacturers were confused as to the author's needs as a potential customer:

> I don't know if there's been some terrible misunderstanding, where you got the idea that I'd really like the prospect of coming home from work and spending my valuable free time taking part in your stupid idea about sausages, or tea, or washing bloody powder, or pretty much anything else for that matter. But here's the thing. I don't. I don't want to make a *film*, or draw a picture, or nominate a friend. Or compose a soundtrack or re-edit your advert. Really, I don't.[28]

It serves as good warning that because people can create does not mean that they want to make advertisements for brands and agencies. As ever, the onus is on brands to find compelling ways to earn atten-tion. An obvious and simple mechanic that addresses the barrier to participation is something of enough value to the audience you want to engage with. When we created the 5.9-second film festival, embracing brevity and highlighting the 0–60 acceleration speed of a BMW 3 Series, all we had to do was offer a BMW 3 Series as a prize in order to get thousands of entries. (It seemed almost prophetic when the Twitter product Vine, a six-second film-sharing app, launched the following year.)

Back to the future of planning advertising

Inherent to the concept of planning is looking forward at what is now a rapidly moving inherently unpredictable network of inter-operating elements, leading people to embrace a portfolio 'many little fires' approach to advertising.

This model makes sense when thinking of creative products released into the protean network, but a 90+ per cent failure rate is not commercially sustainable for agencies in totality. The whole point of planning is to get better odds of success by basing ideas on something. Some agencies are calling this 'data-driven creativity', using data (and presumably insights from the data) to increase their chances of success.

Of course, this is what planners have always done.

Content scarcity has given way to overload, fixed channels dissolved into fluid networks, and audiences have become participants in consumer-driven conversations. This shift requires a new course of action for brands; it demands new marketing imperatives and gives pause to those tasked with making the work *work*.

If we return to the roots of planning we see at its heart a desire to understand human behaviour and provide a robust model for influencing it. Rather than dismantling strategy into endless experimentation, we need a new way of understanding the world, a modern philosophy. In light of all the challenges to established thinking, the response from planning must not be an abandonment of trying to understand, lest we accept that not only have we been wrong, but we can never be right.

As Rachel Hatton, strategy partner at Dare, has pointed out: 'There was a lot of thinking about how communication worked in the 1960s and 1970s. It feels like, now, it's all practice and no theory. If we want to professionalise as an industry, we need to pay more attention to how communication actually works in this new world.'[29]

The emergence of a new media system is typified by a period of transposition, where the grammar of the previous system remains dominant. The first television shows were radio shows with people talking directly into camera. The first films were stage plays that had been filmed. The first marketing forays online took what we knew about media and branding from broadcast media and applied it to a whole new space – but digital is different.

Digital is not a channel. It is a suite of platforms, channels and tactics that will, ultimately, subsume media entirely. Digital marketing is not simply a new place to disperse symbols but rather the emergence of a new behavioural grammar for companies, as they begin to engage with their customers in new ways in new spaces, where everyone has an equal voice.

Prospection
Planning for the future we want

Prospection, the act of looking forward in time, is a quintessentially human endeavour.

Some consider it *the* quintessential human endeavour: 'The human being is the only animal that thinks about the future.'[1]

The philosopher Daniel Dennett notes that 'the fundamental purpose of brains is to produce future... brains are, in essence, anticipation machines'.[2] We spend much of our time projecting forward and we do this to motivate ourselves to reach towards our desired future, using the lens of that future as a way to understand what we should be doing now.

Mankind is characterized by its nature as a planner.

Advertising has begun to wring its hands and discuss more its own future as things change faster. This is an expression of the industry's desire to steer its own path into the future: as Alan Kay said, the best way to predict the future is to invent it.[3] We can motivate ourselves by imagining less pleasant tomorrows, of eroding relevance and margins, and thus engage in prudent, prophylactic behaviour now.

Ideas versus utterances

We sell ideas but we conflate ideas with articulations, concept with craft.

This is dangerous because the nature of what could be deemed advertising is changing rapidly and, as we know, advertising is a means, not an end. This leaves us open to being unable to compete amongst new varieties of solution that are increasingly important:

What is a Big Idea not? It's not a TV script. It's not a key visual. It's not an iPhone app. It's not a QR code. It's not a Facebook app. It's not a tactic. A Big Idea is a thought that keeps giving. A Big Idea is a world you can occupy and keep drawing on.[4]

Low latency communication

One smart response to the diminished latency of culture is low latency advertising – work that responds to actions in one part of the media system in other parts of that system, in approaching real time.

CASE STUDY

The Old Spice Response campaign took a low latency approach and used it to win the internet for a couple of days. This was a follow-up to the incredibly successful Man Your Man Could Smell like spot,[5] featuring Isaiah Mustafa as the eponymous man, which was launched online just *before* Super Bowl 2010 (and not on television *during* it, despite what people misremember). This was a hijack campaign, designed to counter the launch of Dove Men+Care, which had bought Super Bowl airtime. Old Spice bought Super Bowl-related search terms to inject their film into the Super Bowl advertising conversation.

The Old Spice Response campaign was based on a very simple idea: what if the Old Spice man responded to tweets, on YouTube? And so he did, for three days, replying to questions and comments from the great and interesting on Twitter, making short comedic response videos. The vertically integrated production team at Wieden+Kennedy wrote and made a total of 186 short films in those three days. It garnered more than 1 billion earned impressions and made Old Spice the all-time most viewed sponsored channel on YouTube.[6]

Alacrity is the key here – being able not just to move fast, but to *respond* fast.

After that, Kraft solicited ideas, turned a tweet into a TV spot and got it on air the same day during the Conan late night show on the US channel TBS.[7]

It is not just the speed – the low latency aspect – that is interesting, it is the reversal of polarity.

Advertising history note

In Jon Steel's excellent book *Truth, Lies and Advertising* (1998), he relates the tale of Goodby's campaign for Chevy's Mexican restaurants.

They had a line 'Fresh Mex' that Goodby Silverstein & Partners brought to life by shooting ads and getting them on air the same day.

That was in 1991.

Social TV

I don't know what TV is anymore.

JAY LENO[8]

Television is an assemblage, one that is only getting more confusion with the newly minted term 'social TV'.

What is social TV? It remains a semantic battleground as old and new media collide in the living room, each seeking to be dominant. The television industry, having defended its closed network thus far, has begun to realize that opening up to the rest of the system provides an opportunity to regain the cultural salience and create more truly shared viewing experiences in real time – the new water cooler effect.[9]

People use social media to find shows, to find other people to watch with and to comment on shows. They may not turn on their TV there and then just because of something they have seen on social media, though 12 per cent of people claim to have done just that.[10] Even more (17 per cent) claim to have started to watch a show because of something they have seen on social media, and nearly double (30 per cent) have continued watching a programme because of social media commentary.[11]

Perhaps inevitably, these conversations begin to interact with the TV content. Multi-screen viewing and the ability to connect via the social web is driving an increase in television viewing, with users using the secondary screens to enhance the content or experience of viewing.

'Backchannel conversations are happening, with or without marketers. Gone are the days of couch potatoes; social TV has sparked a movement of active and engaged consumers', wrote my wife Rosie for Digiday, when she was working with Bravo.[12]

One of the earliest examples of brands tapping into this idea came from MTV show *The Hills* with backchannel, which let viewers exchange snarky comments in real time while watching the show. A host of different start-ups have since emerged looking to formalize the grammar, and provide the preferred platform for social TV, but none have been as successful as Twitter, which seems a natural successor to the water cooler.

Reverse the polarity

For the less geeky reader, 'reversing the polarity' is a *deus ex machina* device commonly deployed in *Star Trek*, *Doctor Who* and other sci-fi series, especially where forcefields and advanced energy drives are common. It is the last-minute solution that always solves problems because, for some reason, future technology works better when you route the flow of energy through it backwards.

Tweets are appearing in advertisements all over the place, which is part of what I mean by reversing the polarity. Trident ran a print ad featuring real tweets. Wheat Thins made YouTube videos where they tracked down fans who had mentioned them on Twitter and delivered a truckload of Wheat Thins to them.

Informing broadcast with social, rather than looking at the social activation of broadcast. Embracing real people, real stuff, real voices. Increasingly, I suspect, broadcast will be used to reflect what is happening in other parts of the media system.

Why?

- Because people like being listened to (appreciation).
- Because people believe other people (endorsement).
- Because one of the reasons people engage with brands is to acquire fame (fame).
- Because the system allows it and what can be done should be tried (experimentation).
- Because, like social TV, it brings salience and real-time relevance to a time-shifted, fragmented medium (cut-through).
- Because it reflects how people are consuming media, watching TV and being online at the same time, tweeting and talking (media design).
- Because the new model of marketing is to do stuff *for* people and then tell everyone else about it with advertising (solutions, not propositions).

(Whew.)

Which is the other part of what I mean by reversing the polarity:

- Advertising used to tell you how brands could solve your problems.
- Now it needs to solve problems and tell you about it, because everyone knows how most products work.

Beyond the tweet

Reversing the polarity is not simply about pulling tweets into other channels. That has just been one of the easiest ways to create dynamic content experiences that react to changes in the system. The larger opportunity comes from understanding that media is one system, and that people like it when brands respond to them, publicly.

We can entirely reverse the historical polarity of advertising media. Rather than trickle down television, we build up from fragments of many conversations, crafting broadcast stories around real people. The most interesting can then be deployed in broadcast media.

One example of this way of thinking is the Domino's Turnaround campaign. The campaign starts with real customers expressing why they don't like Domino's pizza. This leads to a new pizza recipe and an advertising campaign centred on finding the original research attendees and taking them the new recipe for their honest response. Whilst obviously a staged experiment, it is a dramatization of a reverse polarity approach.

This spread to the packaging, where pizza proverbs from customers were inscribed on the boxes and the menus, which incorporated pictures submitted by customers, rather than staged food shots.

The key thing is for brands to listen to what people are saying and then incorporate what they say, and solutions and surprises to delight them, into content and behaviour.

New principles of planning

The planning of advertising must be about rigour, understanding and inspiration. It must constantly evolve as our understanding of behaviour and culture evolves. As Mark Pollard wrote, it is 'important to acknowledge that what account planners do is part-science, part-intuition. However, it's the intuition that makes a planner stand out.'[13]

But building from beliefs, we can proceed as follows:

- How do we create value?

- How do we understand participants and passives, actions and channels?

- How do we inspire brand behaviour, not just brand utterances?

As Feldwick points out, all aspects of brand behaviour are communicative, and human communication is always about relationships, and less about message transmission than we believe.

The types of 'meta-communication' most successful in building relationships are reciprocal (solving problems for people) or imitative (creating behaviours that can be copied). The kinds of ideas that earn attention in an infinite media space are likely to require understanding of participation – users rather than audiences – and context.

People are not simply customers or prospects, because customers are not the same as people. *Customers are to people as waves are to water.*

'Customers' are a repeating pattern of behaviour that expresses itself in people. Successful ideas create customers by modifying behaviour. Conscious or subconscious attention needs to be aggregated at scale to modify enough behaviour to create significant commercial impact. Ideas spread or die in the attention market.

A new planning toolkit

There can be only one strategy

As we have discussed already, the industry has conflated 'planning' and 'strategy'. Business strategy directs how companies should marshal finite resources to achieve business objectives and achieve profitable growth; it does not assume advertising campaigns as an output, which account planning – at least within traditional agencies – is usually required to do. Strategy must be holistic.

Systems architecture

The multimodal complexity of the mediascape requires more than putting the same idea in many places. It necessitates an integrative system design approach that establishes the priorities and interoperation of elements. This needs to combine the silos of media and advertising, understanding content and context, as well as embracing participation, social behaviour and the impact of technology.

Socially generated actions are increasingly important in a world where consumer broadcast networks are supplanting broadcast ones. Algorithms like Facebook's indicate that content people engage with will be disseminated more efficiently.

Content is necessary but not sufficient. Everyone is making content all the time, which presents new kinds of challenges for 'commercial meaning makers' for achieving salience in an infinite space. Content creation and distribution can no longer be the only tool we use.

Brands are behavioural templates

A brand for a company is like a reputation for a person. You earn reputation by trying to do hard things well.

JEFF BEZOS, FOUNDER OF AMAZON.COM [14]

There are two ways to understand the relationship between 'person-ality' and 'behaviour': either actions are identity *reflective* – in that everything you do is an expression of some irreducible, unchanging essence that is you; or they are *constitutive*, in that who you are, that essence, is a function of those actions.

I believe in processes, not fixity – like the river of Heraclitus, which you can never cross twice. I think we are constantly evolving, changing, growing and, therefore, I believe in actions as the things that make us who we are. I believe brand actions are identity constitutive not identity reflective, which means that you are what you do, and what you do changes who you are.

Actions beget actions. Strategy informs brand behaviour in totality. As marketers, we should look to aggregate behavioural, rather than misleading cognitive, responses. Google search volume is a far more robust measure of salience than survey-based awareness tracking.

The types of actions should leverage principles of 'meta-communi-cation': reciprocity and social copying. Do things for people – solve a brand problem by solving consumer problems. Introduce intermediate behaviours for imitation. Create content that people find valuable, give them tools they can use. Leverage advertising creation and dis-tribution to help disseminate – 'ideas that can be advertised', not just advertising ideas. [15]

The new briefing

The advertising brief is one of the key artefacts in an agency process. It encapsulates the strategy and serves as the guide and yardstick for the creative work and the production it initiates. The standard advertising brief dates back to at least the emergence of planning, and almost always answers these questions:

- What is the problem, or opportunity?
- Who are we talking to?
- What should the advertising achieve?
- What is the single thought we want to leave the audience with?
- What will make them believe this?

The form and content of the brief has been remarkably stable, as it moved through the industry across agencies and decades. This is problematic for several reasons. One of the ironies of advertising, evidenced by the lack of differentiation in brief formats from different agencies, is that agencies have a hard time differentiating themselves. The irony being, of course, that they sell differentiation services to clients that sell functionally parity products.

I was once in a training session with heads of various agencies about winning new business. When it came time for questions, one raised his hand and asked something like this: 'The problem we face is that we offer the same set of services as our competitors, and so find it hard to differentiate during pitches. What is your advice?'

I couldn't contain myself: *You sell that service to clients. Physician heal thyself.*

The problem stems from the fact that many agencies, faced with increasing competition, economic pressure and diminished margins, don't adhere to a set of values as once they did, don't anchor their work and processes to a set of beliefs about how people, the world, business, brands and advertising work. Steve Henry, one of the founders of HHCL, puts it like this:

They did a survey recently of what clients thought of their advertising agency counterparts and the word that came top was *smarmy*... [as in] not having any principles. Bill Bernbach, the brightest man ever to work in our industry, famously said 'a principle isn't a principle until it costs you money'. Most agency chiefs are more like Groucho Marx who said 'These are my principles. If you don't like them, I have others.'[16]

The other problem that the reification of the brief suggests is that is hasn't embraced the fact that things have changed a great deal. As Gareth Kay, former chief strategy officer of GS&P and co-founder of Chapter, has pointed out, all similar briefs make similar assumptions:

- a problem to be solved *with* advertising;
- 'consumers' to 'target';
- a message to say at them;
- reasons to believe;
- tone of voice;
- hopefully some idea of which media have been selected.

(One of the unfortunate aspects of the division between 'creative' agencies and 'media agencies' is that a client may ask for ideas that solve the brief, but will have already committed media spend in certain channels, which dictates the nature of the solution.)

Since the possible creative solutions to a business problem now far extend beyond traditional media placements, and our understanding of human behaviour and decision sciences suggest that rational messaging is not the core element of persuasive communication, I suggest we need a new way to approach briefs.

This is mine, based on what I believe, but it is important to remember that a map is not the territory. A brief is a cognitive tool to help create solutions for clients that work, not a form to be slavishly filled out. As Richard Huntingdon, chief strategy officer of Saatchi & Saatchi London, once commented on my blog: 'Sorry to be so blunt but you write a great brief by having a great idea. I have never had any truck with briefing formats because they turn planners into form fillers.'

Moving away from an assumed messaging approach, which we know is partially based on meta-cognitive errors, briefs will incorporate fresh insight from multiple areas and expand their framework.

> ### TOOLKIT   Questions for a new brief
>
> Briefs can be thought of as both a question or an answer.
> The process is asking for a creative solution to a problem.
> However, the brief to the agency is not the creative brief,
> which needs to establish much tighter parameters. Based on
> research, instinct, budgets, context, objectives – that is to say, strategy –
> the solution space needs to be defined by the creative brief:
>
> - What is brand problem? What are related consumer problems? How
>   can we solve for both?
> - What does success look like? Tangible, measurable?
> - Who are participants and passives?
> - What provocations can we glean from their behaviour?
> - What are the appropriate brand actions and apertures?
> - What is the desired behavioural response?
>
> Figure 11.1 shows a template I created of this brief, which can also be found
> online at: **http://bit.ly/ANEWBRIEF**.

FIGURE 11.1   A new brief format

IN BRIEF	One line summary of the brief		IDEA BRIEF
WHAT NEEDS TO HAPPEN?			
What needs to happen? What's the business challenge and marketing task? Why does this brief exist?			
COMMUNITY INSIGHT	**BRAND INSIGHT**	**CULTURE INSIGHT**	**SOCIAL INSIGHT**
What do we know matters to the community we wish to engage? What do they see as valuable?	*What is the brand's POV? How does it behave in the world? What makes it special? What does it do that no one else does?*	*What is the relevant element of culture to tap into? The tension that can be solved? The movement that can be harnessed / created?*	*What is being discussed in social media about this brand and topic? Who are the influential voices? What is the sentiment?*
BRAND ACTION		**BRAND TERRITORY**	
What's the key thing the brand wishes to do for the community? How will it stimulate conversations and participation? How is it verbing?		*What are the key media for this community? What are the best channels for achieving the business objectives? What media should we create? What should we not overlook?*	
WHAT IS THE KEY BEHAVIOUR WE WISH TO CREATE?			
What do we want the community to do? Be as specific as possible. If it is buy more frequently – when, and for what? Are there intermediate behaviours that will help gauge successful engagement with the community? Google searches (what terms), social activity, store traffic, social media volume.			

Briefing is a collaborative process and the process is as important as the document, as are the dynamics of the groups involved. Generative propositions that inform actions and apertures, relevant inspiration, a collaborative environment and a strong point of view are all factors in helping to concept and craft successful ideas.

Marketing as social experiment

CASE STUDY

An approach embracing actions, ads, content and tools was instrumental in the development of the launch campaign for BMW's first electric vehicle, the ActiveE. Working as one of both the strategy and creative directors on this, I have a particularly holistic view of its development.

The launch had a number of elements that made it challenging. The electric vehicle (EV) was to be a limited field test in the United States and communication needed to begin more than a year before the car would be available, due to competitive pressure in the market. The core BMW driver is motivated by performance but that wasn't something we could guarantee here. As a beta product it might have glitches, indeed the purpose of the field trial was to road-test the new design, to inform development on the mass electric vehicles coming down the line.

On a field-test-sized launch budget we needed to collate a relevant customer base. The initial thinking at the time led towards a green positioning. The Nissan Leaf, clearly named using such a strategy, had just launched. However, greenwashing from too many brands had begun to create a backlash. Indeed, we found a way to position against the market this way. Sustainability, as a movement, by its very definition, could be understood as holding things back:

> You don't want your marriage to be sustainable. You want it to be evolving, nurturing, learning.[17]

So we would position the ActiveE as a symbol of progress, not sustainability. The customer base we needed would consist of people who had a beta-tester mindset, who wouldn't mind any problems the car might have. Rather, the motivation comes from early access and a desire to be involved in making things better. Participants in the future of mobility. We called them *Electronauts* and would work with them for the next few years.

The entire programme was conceived as a social experiment, a collective engineering project that would help to inform next generation cars. The pioneers we needed to court considered themselves well informed, and looked to learn things from niche media before the rest of the world hears about it. Thus, traditional advertising would have been strategically incorrect and wasteful.

First we began a relevant content-driven conversation around the core topics of mobility, design and technology in order to attract the appropriate community. We created a series of films for and of the web, short hypertextual fragments, under the banner we created: BMW Documentaries. There were 25 influential voices invited to take part, including Marissa Mayer (formerly of Google, now CEO of Yahoo!), Buzz Aldrin (yes, the astronaut), Chris Anderson (then editor of *Wired* magazine), Naveen Selvadurai (one of the founders of Foursquare) and Robin Chase (the founder of Zipcar) – all of whom were given free rein to express their points of view, whether or not it aligned with BMW's. They also helped to distribute the content using their own social footprint.

The films were seeded as content exclusives online, appearing as content in the appropriate environments for the community we wanted to create, including *Wired* and *The Atlantic*. The films led us to the second phase, creating a tool for drivers considering buying an EV. One of the big barriers to adoption that we uncovered was 'range anxiety', an irrational fear of being caught short without a way to charge the car, despite the fact that it will go 100 miles on a single charge (and the vast majority of Americans drive less than 40 miles each day). So we created a mobile phone application and corresponding web dashboard to let users track their own drives and assuage their fears: 'How clever is an app that lets consumers track their driving habits and daily driving distances to assuage their trepidation about driving a battery-powered car?'[18]

BMW received 11 times more applications for the car than were available, and all were leased in less than two months. The final phase continued, highlighting the stories of these drivers, using their real voices and passion to continue to build excitement for the coming range of electric vehicles, just as the data from the cars and app would help to build those cars.

Innovative work *works*, for the client and the agency. The agency went on to win more awards, in multiple categories, for that than for any other piece of work from the previous five years.

Where do *you* want to go?

The future of the industry comes down to understanding the seemingly simple answer to the question: what business are we in?

Since advertising is a lever, it follows that if we find a better one we should use it. Buying attention is no longer sufficient, no one has enough money to out-shout the rest of culture. Advertising used to work simply because it could reliably garner enough attention. Now the need to leverage creativity and make difficult strategic choices about how to allocate time and money has never been greater.

Advertising is in no way dead. Indeed, the advertising agency structure is perfectly suited for a complex age. Since agencies separate ideas from executions, an agency can, in theory, work to create any kind of idea, as long as it is capable of *having* that kind of idea.

Agencies are not dead. What is dead is an agency process that can only end in traditional advertising. The world is too complex for that to work for every problem. Ultimately, agencies will embrace a broader palette and work with clients to create value using creativity, in whatever is the most appropriate form.

If strategic planning is able to navigate and guide that transition, if agencies are in the business of profitable brand growth, if they can help brands to behave in new ways, if they have the breadth of vision clients need – then the future of advertising is bright.

At least for those paying attention.

Epilogue
Talkin' about your generation

Generations seem to turn over pretty fast.

Well, technically I guess they don't, since you need to be born during a certain arbitrarily defined time period to be X or Y or whatever.

I recently saw an article that indicated that I was a millennial. This confused me, since I had always known myself to be a tail-end member of Generation X. Since the dates are arbitrary, different sources use different years. I suddenly wondered if I had been 'disaffected' at all, and whether I should be more 'entitled', since the media suggest these are the defining adjectives of that generation. Then I remembered something that Clay Shirky once said: that defining cohorts is functionally equivalent to writing horoscopes, except about decades rather than months.

In *Being Digital*, Negroponte says that 'each generation will be more digital than the last',[1] and *media generations* turn over faster and faster, as new media emerge. This is worth remembering. Whether you consider yourself a digital immigrant or native, keep in mind that being native now is not what will be native soon. And I mean very soon. You have to run to keep up with an accelerating culture.

With this rate of change, when I'm asked for advice by people getting into the industry, I try to make it useful by being vague, because only principles will have longevity in a time of flux:

- Be nice. All the time. To everyone.

- Try to meet other nice people who are interested in the same things as you.

- Equally, converse with people who have different points of view.

- Don't be afraid to change your mind.

- Don't get (too) cynical.

- Stay interested in what you do.

- Stay interested in other things too.

- Never be afraid to ask questions.

- Reading is for awesome people.

- Write.

- Take pictures.

- Develop your own theory about how ideas work and what they are for – but don't fall in love with it.

- Become a geek or an expert on something – *anything*.

- Steal everything – every trick and idea – and make them your own.

- Travel to other parts of the world, especially places that are hard to get to.

- *Have fun*. Seriously. If it isn't any fun, it won't be any good.

- Don't worry too much – it's only advertising, after all.

Trust me, the future will be awesome.

REFERENCES

Introduction

1 Shakespeare, W (1991) *Julius Caesar*, Act III, Scene II, Dover Publications, USA

2 Mashon, Michael [accessed 19 November 2014], *Sponsor* [Online] http://www.museum.tv/eotv/sponsor.htm

3 Wolfe, John [accessed 19 November 2014] GroupM Forecasts 2012 Global ad Spending to Increase 6.4% [Online] http://www.wpp.com/wpp/press/2011/dec/05/groupm-forecasts-global-ad-spending-to

4 Siegle, MG [accessed 19 November 2014] Eric Schmidt: Every 2 Days We Create as Much Information as We Did Up To 2003 [Online] http://techcrunch.com/2010/08/04/schmidt-data/

5 Shirky, C (2011) *Cognitive Surplus: How technology makes consumers into collaborators*, Penguin Books, Reprint edition, UK

6 Dyson, Esther [accessed 19 November 2014] The Rise of the Attention Economy [Online] http://www.aljazeera.com/indepth/opinion/2012/12/20121227113275429.html

7 Lives of 8- to 18-Year-Olds [Online; no longer available] http://www.kff.org/entmedia/entmedia012010nr.cfm

8 Bindley, Katherine (21 March 2012) [accessed 25 November 2014] ADHD Diagnoses in Children Up 66 Percent [Online] http://www.huffingtonpost.com/2012/03/21/adhd-diagnoses-up-by-66-perent_n_1370793.html

9 Mahdawi, Arwa (19 August 2014) [accessed 25 November 2014] Satire is Dying Because the Internet is Killing It [Online] http://www.theguardian.com/commentisfree/2014/aug/19/satire-tag-internet-killing-facebook-tag (The research itself is a little spurious in its conclusions, but it gives a sense of the pervasive feeling of the time.)

10 Shannon, C and Weaver, W (1971) *The Mathematical Theory of Communication*, University of Illinois Press, USA

11 Gilbert, D (2007) *Stumbling on Happiness*, p 215, Vintage, USA

12 Sunstein, Cass (28 April 2008) [accessed 25 November 2014] Solidarity in Consumption [Online] http://papers.ssrn.com/sol3/papers.cfm?abstract_id=224618

13 This maxim is often attributed to Jesus Christ, but is much older, recorded at least as far back as 500 BC in *Analects of Confucius*, chapter 15, verse 23

14 Heath, D and Heath, C (2007) *Made to Stick*, p 12, Random House, USA

15 Frommer, D and Kamelia, A [accessed 25 November 2014] Chart of the Day: Half Of YouTube Videos Get Fewer Than 500 Views [Online] http://www.businessinsider.com/chart-of-the-day-youtube-videos-by-views-2009-5

16 Green, Adam (7 January 2013) [accessed 25 November 2014] A Pickpocket's Tale, The spectacular thefts of Apollo Robbins [Online] http://www.newyorker.com/reporting/2013/01/07/130107fa_fact_green#ixzz2MK2AqXIV

17 Trost, Matthew (1 March 2010) [accessed 25 November 2014] The Riddle of Experience vs. Memory: Daniel Kahneman on TED.com [Online] http://blog.ted.com/2010/03/01/the_riddle_of_e/

18 James, W (1950) *The Principles of Psychology*, p 403, Dover Publications, USA

19 Macknik, S and Martinez-Conde, S (2011) *Sleights of Mind: What the neuroscience of magic reveals about our everyday deceptions*, p 60, Picador, UK

Chapter 1

1 Bogart, L (1967) *Strategy in Advertising*, Harcourt, Brace & World, Inc, USA

2 Benson, Joseph and Foley, Jack [accessed 25 November 2014] When Banks Merge, What Happens to the Brand? [Online] http://www.brandchannel.com/papers_review.asp?sp_id=620

3 Peters, Tom [accessed 25 November 2014] Brandweek Article Quoted in The State of the US Consumer Report, *Saatchi & Saatchi* [Online] http://www.saatchikevin.com/workingit/myra_stark_report.html

4 Pavitt, J (2002) *Brand New*, p 14, V & A Publications, UK

5 Peters, Tom (10 August 2011) [accessed 25 November 2014] The Brand Called You [Online] http://www.fastcompany.com/online/10/brandyou.html

6 Geoghegan, Tom (9 November 2005) [accessed 25 November 2014] A Child Called Ikea: Myth or Reality [Online] http://news.bbc.co.uk/2/hi/uk_news/magazine/4418934.stm

7 Kay, John (6 December 1996) [accessed 25 November 2014] *What's in a name?* [Online] http://www.johnkay.com/1996/12/06/whats-in-a-name

8 Post on Chav Scum website [accessed 2010] [Online, no longer available] http://www.chavscum.co.uk/forum/archive/index.php/t-7132.html

9 Pavitt, J (2002) *Brand New*, p 23, V & A Publications, UK

10 Armstrong, K (2006) *A Short History of Myth*, p 4, Canongate US, USA

11 Duckworth, G (1996) Brands and the role of advertising, in *Understanding Brands*, ed Don Cowley, p 68, Kogan Page, UK

12 Grant, J (2000) *The New Marketing Manifesto*, p 15, Texere, UK

13 Ibid

14 Armstrong, K (2006) *A Short History of Myth*, p 119, Canongate US, USA

15 Klages, M [accessed 25 November 2014] Claude Levi-Strauss: The Structural Study of Myth [Online] http://www.colorado.edu/English/ENGL2012Klages/levi-strauss.html

16 Levi Strauss, Claude (1976) Structural Anthropology Volume 2, University of Chicago Press, USA

17 Holt, D (2003) What Becomes an Icon Most?, p4, *Harvard Business Review*, reprint, USA

18 Doward, Jamie and Teuscher, Lea (25 September 2005) [accessed 25 November 2014] Tobacco firms' subtle tactics lure smokers to their brand [Online] http://www.theguardian.com/media/2005/sep/25/advertising.smoking

19 Levi Strauss, Claude (1967) *The Structural Study of Myth: Structural anthropology*, trans. Claire Jacobsen and Brooke Scheoff, Doubleday Anchor Books, New York

20 Duckworth, Gary (January 1995) [accessed 28 November 2014] How Advertising Works, the Universe and Everything, *Admap* [Online] http://www.warc.com/Search/advertising%20works/advertising%20works.warc?q=advertising+works&Area=Articles&Tab=

21 www.welcometoplanet3.com [accesssed via Wayback Machine 25 November 2014] [Online] https://web.archive.org/web/20041215021901/ http://www.welcometoplanet3.com/home.html

22 Klein, N (2009) *No Logo*, p22, Picador, USA

23 Klein, N (2009) *No Logo*, p52, Picador, Carmine Collection, USA

24 BRANDZ [accessed 25 November 2014] Google Ranked 1st in MB Brandz 100 Top Brands Report 2014 [Online] https://mb.brandz.com/

25 Bing [Online] http://www.bingiton.com/

26 'Googol' is the mathematical term for a 1 followed by 100 zeros. The term was coined by Milton Sirotta, nephew of American mathematician Edward Kasner, and was popularized in the book, *Mathematics and the Imagination*, by Kasner and James Newman. Google's play on the term reflects the company's mission to organize the immense amount of information available on the web [Online] http://www.google.com/corporate/index.html

27 Google, Code of Conduct [Online] http://investor.google.com/conduct.html

28 Willigan, Geraldine (July 1992) [accessed 25 November 2014] High Performance Marketing, Interview with Phil Knight [Online] https://hbr.org/1992/07/high-performance-marketing-an-interview-with-nikes-phil-knight

29 Feldwick, P (2002) *What is Brand Equity, Anyway?*, NTC Publications, UK

30 Bullmore, Jeremy (2002) [accessed 25 November 2014] Posh Spice & Persil: The Value of Fame [Online] http://www.wpp.com/wpp/marketing/branding/articles-poshspice/. Here, Jeremy Bullmore argues that every corporate action and decision influences people's perceptions of brands

31 Ibid

32 For more on the private language argument, see L Wittgenstein (1953) *Philosophical Investigations*, Wiley-Blackwell, UK

33 WPP.com [accessed 25 November 2014] What is Brand Voltage? [Online] http://www.wpp.com/wpp/marketing/brandz/brand-voltage/

34 Brown, Millward [accessed 25 November 2014] Methodology [Online] http://www.millwardbrown.com/BrandZ/Top_100_Global_Brands/Methodology.aspx

35 WPP.com (2014) [accessed 25 November 2014] BrandZ Top 100 Most Valuable Global Brands 2014 [Online] http://www.wpp.com/wpp/marketing/brandz/brandz-2014/

36 Ehrenberg, Andrew and Goodhardt, Gerald (January 2002) [accessed 25 November 2014] Double Jeopardy Revisited, Again [Online] http://marketingscience.info/assets/documents/163/7618.pdf

37 Paynter, Ben (6 January 2013) [accessed 25 November 2014] Suds For Drugs [Online] http://nymag.com/news/features/tide-detergent-drugs-2013-1/

38 Ibid

39 Fera, Rae Ann [accessed 25 November 2014] The Rise of Sadvertising, Why Brands are Determined to Make You Cry [Online] http://www.fastcocreate.com/3029767/the-rise-of-sadvertising-why-brands-are-determined-to-make-you-cry#!

40 Legro, Tom (3 February 2014) [accessed 25 November 2014] Thursday's NewsHour: Joyce Carol Oates Tells 'A Widow's Story' [Online] http://www.pbs.org/newshour/art/thursdays-newshour-joyce-carol-oates-tells-widows-tale/

41 P&G (2012) [accessed 25 November 2014] P&G – Thank You Mama – Best Job 2012 HD 2M [Online] http://www.youtube.com/watch?v=0ruHOaHrGnQ

42 Dove (14 April 2013) [accessed 25 November 2014] Dove Real Beauty Sketches [Online] http://www.youtube.com/watch?v=litXW91UauE

43 Schacter, D (1997) *Searching For Memory*, Basic Books, USA

Chapter 2

1 Heath, R (2012) *Seducing the Subconscious: The psychology of emotional influence in advertising*, Wiley-Blackwell, USA

2 Heath, RG and Hyder, P (2005) Measuring the hidden power of emotive advertising, *International Journal of Market Research*, 47 (5), pp 467–86

3 Psychoanalysis [Online] en.wikipedia.org/wiki/Psychoanalysis

4 Wegner, Daniel (February 2003) [accessed 25 November 2014] *The Mind's Best Tricks: How We Experience Conscious Will* [Online] http://www.wjh.harvard.edu/~wegner/pdfs/trick.pdf

5 Shah, Hetan and Dawney, Emma [accessed 25 November 2014] Behavioural Economics, New Economics Foundation [Online] http://www.neweconomics.org/publications/entry/behavioural-economics

6 Earls, Mark (2003) [accessed 25 November 2014] Advertising to the Herd: How Understanding Our True Nature Challenges the Ways We Think about Advertising and Market Research [Online] http://www.uvm.edu/~pdodds/teaching/courses/2009-08UVM-300/docs/others/2003/earls2003a.pdf

7 Lattin, James, Ortmeyer, Gwendolyn and Montgomery, David (1987) [accessed 25 November 2014] Routinized Choice Behavior, Brand Commitment, and Consumer Response to Promotions [Online] https://gsbapps.stanford.edu/researchpapers/library/RP935.pdf

8 Gordon, W (2003) Brands on the Brain, in *Brand New Brand Thinking*, ed M Baskin and M Earls, Kogan Page, UK

9 Earls, M (2003) Learning to live without the Brand, in *Brand New Brand Thinking*, ed M Baskin and M Earls, Kogan Page, UK

10 Levitt, S and Dubner, S (2009) *Freakonomics*, p 84, Harper Perennial, USA

11 Graves, P (2010) *Consumer.ology*, Nicholas Brealey Publishing, USA

12 Smell & Taste Treatment and Research Foundation Ltd [accessed 25 November 2014] [Online] http://www.smellandtaste.org/

13 Graves, P (2010) *Consumer.ology*, Nicholas Brealey Publishing, USA

14 Gladwell, M (2007) *Blink*, p 81, Back Bay Books, USA

15 Fishbein, M and Ajzen, I (1975) *Belief, Attitude, Intention, and Behaviour: An introduction to theory and research*, Addison-Wesley Pub (Sd), USA

16 Ball, P (2006) *Critical Mass: How one thing leads to another*, p 395, Farrar, Straus and Giroux, USA

17 Business Week (4 June 2006) [accessed 25 November 2014] The Science of Desire [Online] http://www.businessweek.com/stories/2006-06-04/the-science-of-desire

18 Ethnography [Online] http://en.wikipedia.org/wiki/Ethnography

19 Observer-expectancy effect [Online] http://en.wikipedia.org/wiki/Observer_bias

20 Millward Brown [Online] http://www.millwardbrown.com/theadvertisedmind/copytesting.html

21 Feldwick, Paul [accessed 25 November 2014] TV and the Brain [Online] http://www.thinkbox.tv/server/show/nav.1135

22 Feldwick, Paul [accessed 25 November 2014] Exploding the Message Myth [Online] http://www.thinkbox.tv/server/show/nav.1015

23 Binet, Les and Field, Peter (June 2009) [acccessed 25 November 2014] Empirical Generalisations about Advertising Campaign Success [Online] http://farisyakob.typepad.com/files/binet-field-ipa-databank-empirical-generalizations-about-advertising-campaign-success.pdf

24 Green, Laurence (June 2012) [accessed 25 November 2014] Think Tank: Target consumers' 'unconscious' and reap the rewards [Online] http://www.telegraph.co.uk/finance/businessclub/management-advice/9307587/Think-Tank-Target-consumers-unconscious-and-reap-the-rewards.html

25 United Breaks Guitars (6 July 2009) [accessed 23 November 2014] [Online] http://www.youtube.com/watch?v=5YGc4zOqozo

26 United Breaks Guitars [Online] http://en.wikipedia.org/wiki/United_Breaks_Guitarscite_note-15#

27 Wheaton, K (9 July 2009) [accessed 25 November 2014] United Is Happy to Answer Your Complaints After You Humiliate Them [Online] http://adage.com/article/adages/united-airlines-happy-answer-complaints-humiliation/137817/

28 Esterl, Mike (1 December 2011) [accessed 25 November 2014] A Frosty Reception for Coca-Cola's White Christmas Cans, *Wall Street*

Journal [Online] http://online.wsj.com/news/articles/SB100014240529 702040120045770705212 11375302

29 Stone, Brad (24 September 2010) [accessed 25 November 2014] How Facebook Sells Your Friends [Online] http://www.nbcnews.com/ id/39325170/ns/business-bloomberg_businessweek/

30 Gladwell, M (2002) *The Tipping Point*, Back Bay Books, USA

31 Otero-Millan, Jorge, Macknik, Stephen, Robbins, Apollo and Martinez-Conde, Susana (21 November 2011) [accessed 25 November 2014] Stronger Misdirection in Curved than in Straight Motion [Online] http://www.ncbi.nlm.nih.gov/pmc/articles/PMC3221472/

32 Sony Bravia-Balls (Hi-Res) (1 May 2008) [accessed 28 November 2014] [Online] http://www.youtube.com/watch?v=-zOrV-5vh1A

33 Burley, Jonathan (24 May 2012) [accessed 25 November 2014] [Online] http://www.campaignlive.co.uk/features/1133432/

34 JCast Business News (28 April 2006) [accessed 25 November 2014] Thanks Bravia, Sony Gains Profit [Online] http://en.j-cast.com/ 2006/04/28001215.html

Chapter 3

1 Dyson, P (March 2008) [accessed 25 November 2014] Cutting Adspend in a Recession Delays Recovery [Online] http:// www.gem-online.de/pdf/news/DysonCuttingadspendWARC.pdf

2 Heath, R (2001) *The Hidden Power of Advertising*, NTC Publications, UK

3 Nevill Darby, quoted in Giep Franzen (2003) Advertising frameworks, in *Brand New Brand Thinking*, ed M Baskin and M Earls, Kogan Page, UK

4 Nelson, Emily and Ellison, Sarah (21 September 2005) [accessed 25 November 2014] In a Shift, Marketers Beef Up Ad Spending Inside Stores Funky Displays and Lighting, TV Spots in Wal-Mart; Unsettling Madison Avenue [Online] http://online.wsj.com/articles/ SB112725891535046751

5 Earls, M (2003) Learning to live without the brand, in *Brand New Brand Thinking*, ed M Baskin and M Earls, Kogan Page, UK

6 Useem, Jerry (21 March 2005) [accessed 25 November 2014] The Smartest Books We Know, *Fortune Magazine* [Online] http://archive.fortune.com/magazines/fortune/fortune_archive/ 2005/03/21/8254826/index.htm

7 Somatic marker hypothesis [Online] http://psychology.wikia.com/ wiki/Somatic_marker_hypothesis

8 Iyengar, Sheena and Lepper, Mark (2000) [accessed 25 November 2014] When Choice is Demotivating: Can One Desire Too Much of a Good Thing? [Online] http://www.columbia.edu/~ss957/articles/ Choice_is_Demotivating.pdf

9 FMI [accessed 25 November 2014] Supermarket Facts Industry Overview 2013 [Online] http://www.fmi.org/research-resources/ supermarket-facts

10 Chabris, Christopher and Simons, Daniel (1999) [accessed 25 November 2014] The Invisible Gorilla [Online] http:// www.theinvisiblegorilla.com/videos.html

11 Macknik, S and Martinez-Conde, S (2011) *Sleights of Mind: What the neuroscience of magic reveals about our everyday deceptions*, p 60, Picador, UK

12 Simons, Daniel (2000) [accessed 25 November 2014] Change Blindness Blindness: The Metacognitive Error of Overestimating Change-detection Ability [Online] http://www.vanderbilt.edu/ psychhumdev/levin/labpage/papers/LevinMomDrivSim00.pdf

13 *Campaign* magazine (7 October 2005) [accessed 25 November 2014] The Greatest Agencies of All Time [Online] http://www.campaignlive.co.uk/news/521174/

14 Glasgow, RDV (1995) *Madness, Masks, and Laughter: An essay on comedy*, p 123, Fairleigh Dickinson Univ Press, USA

15 Dobbs, David (June 2007) [accessed 25 November 2014] Big Answers From Little People [Online] http://www.nature.com/scientificamerican/ journal/v17/n2s/full/scientificamerican0607-4sp.html

16 Sleights of Mind [Online] http://www.sleightsofmind.com/

17 Audi – Art of the Heist Case Study (21 November 2010) [accessed 25 November 2014] [Online] https://www.youtube.com/ watch?v=z5w2CNB9clw

18 Sacks, Danielle [accessed 25 November 2014] Down the Rabbit Hole [Online] http://www.fastcompany.com/58038/down-rabbit-hole

19 HighBeam Research (18 January 2008) [accessed 25 November 2014] Movie Review: 'Cloverfield' is a Monster Movie for the YouTube Generation [Online] http://www.highbeam.com/doc/ 1A1-D8U7VC781.html

20 The official *Cloverfield* trailer (9 July 2007) [accessed 25 November 2014] [Online] https://www.youtube.com/watch?v=IvNkGm8mxiM

21 Breznican, Anthony (9 July 2007) [accessed 25 November 2014] Mystifying Trailer Transforms Marketing [Online] http://usatoday30. usatoday.com/life/movies/news/2007-07-08-abrams-trailer_N.htm

22 *Campaign* (12 December 2003) [accessed 25 November 2014] Top Performers of 2003: Campaign of the Year – 118 118 [Online] http://www.campaignlive.co.uk/news/198184/

23 Turner, ES (1952) *The Shocking History of Advertising!*, Michael Joseph, UK

24 The branding blog (7 June 2007) [accessed 25 November 2014] Borrowed Interest Ads Are a Waste [Online] http://thebrandingblog.com/borrowed-interest-ads-are-a-waste/

25 Nielsen (10 April 2012) [accessed 25 November 2014] Consumer Trust in Online, Social and Mobile Advertising Grows [Online] http://www.nielsen.com/us/en/insights/news/2012/consumer-trust-in-online-social-and-mobile-advertising-grows.html

26 *The Simpsons* (2 May 2004) 'Simple Simpson' Episode 19, Season 15 [accessed 25 November 2014] [Online] http://en.wikipedia.org/wiki/The_Simpsons_%28season_15%29

27 Goldhaber, Michael (December 1997) [accessed 25 November 2014] Attention Shoppers! [Online] http://archive.wired.com/wired/archive/5.12/es_attention.html

28 *Creative Computing* (December 1981) [accessed 25 November 2014] Cost of Hard Drive Storage Space [Online] http://ns1758.ca/winch/winchest.html

29 Dumenco, Simon (13 December 2011) [accessed 25 November 2014] Add This: Facebook Makes Up 52% of Sharing on the Web [Online] http://adage.com/article/the-media-guy/facebook-makes-52-sharing-web/231528/

30 Tierney, John (8 February 2010) [accessed 25 November 2014] Will You Be Emailing This Column? It's Awesome [Online] http://www.nytimes.com/2010/02/09/science/09tier.html

31 Ibid

Chapter 4

1 Julian Saunders (2004) Drowning in choice: the revolution in communications planning, *Market Leader*, **24**, pp 34–39

2 Media Implementation, IMC, chapter 32

3 Gross Rating Point [Online] http://en.wikipedia.org/wiki/Gross_rating_point

4 Ibid

5 Vranica, Suzanne (23 March 2014) [accessed 25 November 2014]
A 'Crisis' in Online Ads: One-Third of Traffic Is Bogus [Online] http://
online.wsj.com/news/articles/SB10001424052702304026304579453253860786362

6 Wegert, Tessa (23 August 2012) [accessed 25 November 2014]
What you Need to Know About Viewable Impressions [Online]
http://www.clickz.com/clickz/column/2200135/what-you-need-to-know-about-viewable-impressions

7 Ha, Anthony (14 February 2013) [accessed 25 November 2014]
ComScore Says 5.3 Trillion Ads Shown In 2012, But 3 In 10 Are Never
Seen [Online] http://techcrunch.com/2013/02/14/comscore-digital-future-2013/

8 Collin, Will and Wilkins, John (2000) *The Use of Qualitative Research in Commercial Media Planning, Qualitative Research in Context*,
Admap in conjunction with Association for Qualitative Research (AQR), UK

9 Idea Planning not Channel Planning, presentation to ISBA conference,
Kevin Brown

10 Davies, Russell (1 December 2008) [accessed 25 November 2014]
We're as Disappointed as You Are – Thoughts of a Planner [Online]
http://russelldavies.typepad.com/planning/urban_spam/index.html

11 Baker, S and Michell, H (2000) *Integrated Marketing Communications*,
Routledge, UK

12 Godin, S (1999) *Permission Marketing*, Simon & Schuster, USA

13 Spam [Online] http://www.google.co.uk/search?q=define%3Aspam&start=0&ie=utf-8&oe=utf-8

14 Mirani, Leo (3 September 2013) [accessed 25 November 2014] Over
One-Fifth of People Use Ad-Blocking Software – and it's Beginning to
Hurt [Online] http://qz.com/120797/over-one-fifth-of-people-use-ad-blocking-software-and-its-beginning-to-hurt/

15 Forrester [Online] http://www.forrester.com/ER/Press/Release/0,1769,943,00.html

16 Stephenson, N (1995) *The Diamond Age*, Bantam Spectra, USA

17 Keynote Remarks, Madison + Vine Conference, Steve Heyer, then
COO Coca-Cola

18 iMedia Connection (17 April 2003) [accessed 25 November 2014]
Study Says Spam Affecting All Advertising [Online]
http://www.imediaconnection.com/news/1690.asp

19 IBM [accessed 25 November 2014] The End of Television As We Know It – A Future Industry Perspective [Online] https://www-935.ibm.com/services/us/imc/pdf/ge510-6248-end-of-tv-full.pdf]

20 A phrase coined by Linda Stone, a senior researcher at Microsoft. It is an interesting aside that much of the most insightful thinking about the future of media consumption is being undertaken within technology, and not traditional media, companies.

21 IM and MIT (2002) *Pathways to Measuring Consumer Behaviour in an Age of Media Convergence*, MIT, US

22 Bloom, Jonah (23 April 2006) [accessed 25 November 2014] Media Agencies in Danger of Becoming Obstacles, Not Enablers [Online] http://adage.com/article/jonah-bloom/media-agencies-danger-obstacles-enablers/108739/

23 *Time Magazine* (27 March 2006) Are kids too wired for their own good?, USA

24 Truly, Madly, Deeply Engaged, Yahoo! Summit Series [accessed 25 November 2014] [Online] http://www.ipsos.com/mediact/sites/ipsos.com.mediact/files/pdf/Ipsos_MediaCT-CS_GlobalYouth_MediaTechEngaged.pdf

25 Bullmore, Jeremy (2002) [accessed 25 November 2014] Posh Spice & Persil: The Value of Fame [Online] http://www.wpp.com/wpp/marketing/branding/articles-poshspice/

26 Media Week (17 August 2004) [accessed 25 November 2014] What Marketing Directors Love [Online] http://www.mediaweek.co.uk/article/516346/marketing-directors-love

27 Bullmore, Jeremy (2002) [accessed 25 November 2014] Posh Spice & Persil: The Value of Fame [Online] http://www.wpp.com/wpp/marketing/branding/articles-poshspice/

28 Pine, J and Gilmore, J (1999) *The Experience Economy, Work Is Theater & Every Business a Stage*, Harvard Business School Press, USA

29 Wikipedia [accessed 25 November 2014] The Gamekillers [Online] http://en.wikipedia.org/wiki/The_Gamekillers

30 Visually (10 October 2012) [accessed 25 November 2014] Printer Ink – The most Expensive Liquid in the World [Online] http://visual.ly/printer-ink-most-expensive-liquid-world

31 Redbull.us (7 November 2014) [accessed 25 November 2014] Red Bull Art of Can Chicago [Online] http://www.redbull.com/us/en/events/1331641437090/red-bull-art-of-can-chicago

32 Yakob, Rosie (November 2012) [accessed 25 November 2014] Content Marketing White Paper Rosie Yakob [Online] http://www.360i.com/reports/content-marketing/

33 Griffiths, John (July 2004) [accessed 25 November 2014] Brands as Media [Online] http://www.planningaboveandbeyond.com/downloads/

34 Boyd, Danah (27 May 2014) [accessed 25 November 2014] Selling Out is Meaningless [Online] https://medium.com/message/selling-out-is-meaningless-3450a5bc98d2

35 Kaplan, Melanie (16 May 2010) [accessed 25 November 2014] Stonyfield Farm CEO: How an Organic Yogurt Business Can Scale [Online] http://www.smartplanet.com/blog/pure-genius/stonyfield-farm-ceo-how-an-organic-yogurt-business-can-scale/

36 Durrani, Arif (24 October 2012) [accessed 25 November 2014] Cindy Gallop tells adland: Blow yourselves up and start again [Online] www.campaignlive.co.uk/news/1156423/

37 Feldwick, Paul [accessed 25 November 2014] Exploding The Message Myth by Paul Feldwick [Online] http://www.thinkbox.tv/server/show/nav.1015

38 Ogilvy, D (1985) *Ogilvy on Advertising*, Vintage, UK

Chapter 5

1 Adams, Douglas (29 August 1999) [accessed 25 November 2014] How To Stop Worrying and Learn to Love the Internet [Online] http://www.douglasadams.com/dna/19990901-00-a.html

2 Fiat EcoDrive [Online] http://www.fiat.com/ecodrive/

3 Bestjobs.australia.com [Online] http://www.bestjobs.australia.com/

4 The Best Job in the World [Online] http://en.wikipedia.org/wiki/The_Best_Job_In_The_World

5 Philips (16 April 2009) [accessed 25 November 2014] Carousel Commercial – Adam Berg Commercial of the Year Stink Digital [Online] http://www.youtube.com/watch?v=lQ3D4CqHbJM

6 Negroponte, N (1995) *Being Digital*, Alfred A Knopf, Inc., USA

7 Watts, Duncan (15 April 2007) [accessed 25 November 2014] Is Justin Timberlake a Product of Cumulative Advantage? [Online] http://www.nytimes.com/2007/04/15/magazine/15wwlnidealab.t.html

8 Doctorow, Cory (6 May 2008) [accessed 25 November 2014] Cory Doctorow: Think Like a Dandelion [Online] http://www.locusmag.com/Features/2008/05/cory-doctorow-think-like-dandelion.html

9 Watts, Duncan (15 April 2007) [accessed 25 November 2014] Is Justin Timberlake a Product of Cumulative Advantage? [Online] http://www.nytimes.com/2007/04/15/magazine/15wwlnidealab.t.html

10 Trachtenberg, Jeffrey (22 February 2013) [accessed 25 November 2014] The Mystery of the Book Sales Spike: How Are Some Authors Landing On Best-Seller Lists? They're Buying Their Way [Online] http://online.wsj.com/news/articles/SB10001424127887323864304578 316143623600544

11 Neff, Jack (16 September 2014) [accessed 25 November 2014] How Reckitt Benckiser Became 'Digital at Heart' [Online] http://adage.com/article/cmo-strategy/reckitt-benckiser-digital-heart/294958/

12 Neff, Jack (23 January 2013) [accessed 25 November 2014] Unilever Ad Spending Hits New Heights, But Agency Fees on Downward Trend [Online] http://adage.com/article/news/unilever-ad-spending-hits-heights/239348/

13 Poggi, Jeanine (19 May 2014) [accessed 25 November 2014] The Future of TV? No More Commercials, Says Netflix Chief Product Officer [Online] http://adage.com/article/media/future-tv-commercials-netflix-exec/293275/

Chapter 6

1 Ataque de Pánico! (Panic Attack!) (2009) [accessed 3 November 2009] https://www.youtube.com/watch?v=-dadPWhEhVk

2 Rushkoff, Douglas (2013) *Present Shock: When everything happens now*, Penguin Group, USA

3 Owen, John (4 September 2014) [accessed 25 November 2014] Learning the Hard Way [Online] http://www.campaignlive.co.uk/news/1310419/learning-hard/

4 Ibid

5 Avi, Dan (4 December 2013) [accessed 25 November 2014] What are 10 Great Ad Agencies of 2013, According to CMO's? [Online] http://www.forbes.com/sites/avidan/2013/12/04/ten-great-agencies-of-2013/

6 Dylan, Bolden (5 February 2013) [accessed 25 November 2014] The Digital Road to Earning Travelers' Trust [Online] https://www.bcgperspectives.com/content/interviews/transportation_travel_tourism_digital_economy_bolden_dylan_digital_road_to_earning_travelers_trust/

7 Virgin America [accessed 25 November 2014] [Online] https://www.virginamerica.com/vxnewlook/

8 Mission to the Edge of Space [accessed 25 November 2014] [Online] http://www.redbullstratos.com/

9 Gold, Michael (15 January 2010) [accessed 25 November 2014] Definition 6 Launches Coca-Cola 'Happiness Machine' Video [Online] http://pressrelated.com/press-release-definition-6-launches-coca-cola-happiness-machine-video.html

10 Ho, Adrian (9 September 2014) [accessed 25 November 2014] Platforms, Purpose, and the Future of Marketing [Online] https://www.linkedin.com/today/post/article/20140909140935-3798012-platforms-purpose-and-the-future-of-marketing

11 Ho, Adrian (Partner at Zeus Jones) (9 September 2014) [accessed 25 November 2014] Platforms, Purpose, and the Future of Marketing [Online] http://www.zeusjones.com/blog/2014/platforms-purpose-and-the-future-of-marketing/

12 Ibid

Chapter 7

1 Lehre, J (2010) *How We Decide*, Mariner Books, USA

2 Johnson, S (2011) *Where Good Ideas Come From*, Riverhead Trade, USA

3 Aristotle (350 BCE) *Poetics* (Section 3) [accessed 25 November 2014] [Online] http://classics.mit.edu/Aristotle/poetics.3.3.html

4 Tutton, Mark (1 December 2009) [accessed 25 November 2014] Learn the Five Secrets of Innovation [Online] http://edition.cnn.com/2009/BUSINESS/11/26/innovation.tips/index.html

5 Ibid

6 Erard, Michael (22 May 2004) [accessed 25 November 2014] THINK TANK; Where to Get a Good Idea: Steal It Outside Your Group [Online] http://www.nytimes.com/2004/05/22/arts/22IDEA.htm

7 Ibid

8 *The Categories*, the first logical treatise of Aristotle.

9 Gottfried Wilhelm von Leibniz, quoted in *A Critical Exposition of the Philosophy of Leibniz*, Bertrand Russell (1900) Cambridge University Press, UK

10 Cale, John (12 February 2002) [accessed 25 November 2014] My 15 Minutes, *Guardian* [Online] http://www.theguardian.com/culture/2002/feb/12/artsfeatures.warhol

11 Tate Modern (April 2002) [accessed 25 November 2014 via Wayback Machine] *Warholiser* [Online] http://www.pokelondon.com/portfolio/tate-modern/warholizer/

12 Warhol, A (1977) *The Philosophy of Andy Warhol (From A to B and Back Again)*, Harvest, USA

13 Ibid

14 Bullmore, Jeremy (2002) [accessed 25 November 2014] Posh Spice & Persil: The Value of Fame [Online] http://www.wpp.com/wpp/marketing/branding/articles-poshspice/

15 Eliot, TS (2009) *The Sacred Wood: Essays on Poetry and Criticism*, Dodo Press, UK

16 [Online] https://web.archive.org/web/20080703172252/; http://www.rockhall.com/exhibitpast/lesson-hip-hop/

17 Lethem, Jonathan (February 2007) [accessed 25 November 2014] The Ecstasy of Influence: A plagiarism [Online] http://www.sunydutchess.edu/faculty/allen/lethem%20-%20ecstasy%20of%20influence.pdf

18 PBS Documentary (1966) [accessed 25 November 2014] Triumph of the Nerds: The Rise of Accidental Empires [Online] http://www.pbs.org/nerds/

Chapter 8

1 He was well known for saying it, quoted in Jean Marie Dru (2007) *How Disruption Brought Order*, Palgrave Macmillan, UK

2 To the author, in conversation

3 Nicolson, Nigel [accessed 25 November 2014] Virginia Woolf By Nigel Nicolson [Online] https://www.nytimes.com/books/first/n/nicolson-woolf.html

4 Wilde, O (1993) *De Profundis*, CreateSpace Independent Publishing Platform

5 Kirby, Alan (2006) [accessed 25 November 2014] The Death of Postmodernism and Beyond [Online] https://philosophynow.org/issues/58/The_Death_of_Postmodernism_And_Beyond

6 Ibid

7 Ibid

8 Goldman, David (8 February 2010) [accessed 25 November 2014] Super Bowl Ad Breaks Google's TV Silence [Online] http://money.cnn.com/2010/02/08/technology/google_superbowl_ad/

9 Volkswagen (2 February 2011) [accessed 25 November 2014] The Force: Volkswagen Commercial [Online] https://www.youtube.com/watch?v=R55e-uHQna0

Chapter 9

1 Febreze Breathe Happy Campaign (14 September 2012) [accessed 25 November 2014] [Online] https://www.youtube.com/watch?v=Ea79IcPW47M

2 Brown, Millward (September 2012) [accessed 25 November 2014] 2012 Effie Report, Inaugural Edition [Online] http://www.millwardbrown.com/docs/default-source/insight-documents/articles-and-reports/Effie_Report_2012_Edition.pdf

3 Poulsen, Mai Bruun (9 July 2012) [accessed 25 November 2014] How a Rainbow-Oreo Sparked a Boycott and Doubled the Fan Growth [Online] http://www.mindjumpers.com/blog/2012/07/oreo-boycott/

4 Ibid [Online] http://en.wikipedia.org/wiki/Ibid

5 Binet, Les and Carter, Sarah (November 2010) [accessed 25 November 2014] Mythbusters: Art works [Online] http://www.warc.com/Pages/Search/WordSearch.aspx?q=mythbuster%20art%20works

6 Veksner, Simon (7 May 2008) [accessed 25 November 2014] Tuesday Tip No. 50 – How To Choose Where To Work [Online] http://scampblog.blogspot.com/2008/05/tuesday-tip-no50-how-to-choose-where-to.html

7 See what we did there?

8 London International Awards 2009 [Online] http://en.wikipedia.org/wiki/London_International_Awards

Chapter 10

1 Brown, Celia (22 July 2014) [accessed 25 November 2014] 5 Winning Characteristics of Modern Marketing Teams [Online] http://www.forbes.com/sites/sap/2014/07/22/5-winning-characteristics-of-modern-marketing-teams/

2 Levitt, Theodore (July 2004) [accessed 25 November 2014] Marketing Myopia, *Harvard Business Review* [Online] https://hbr.org/2004/07/marketing-myopia/ar/1

3 Christensen, Clayton, Cook, Scott and Hall, Taddy (December 2005) [accessed 25 November 2014] Marketing Malpractice: The Cause and The Cure [Online] http://hbr.org/web/special-collections/insight/marketing-that-works/marketing-malpractice-the-cause-and-cure

4 Sepe, Veronica (29 March 2011) [accessed 25 November 2014] Television Ad Spending Bounces Back, Virtually Unaffected by Online Growth – eMarketer [Online] http://www.emarketer.com/newsroom/index.php/2011/03/#Y90BrLQtdG7f2SBI.99

5 Kelly, Kevin (2 April 2010) [accessed 25 November 2014] The Shirky Principle [Online] http://kk.org/thetechnium/2010/04/the-shirky-prin/

6 Also called the Growth Share Matrix, developed by the Boston Consulting Group [Online] http://en.wikipedia.org/wiki/Growth%E2%80%93share_matrix

7 Porter five forces analysis – a framework to analyse competition and guide business strategy in an industry [Online] http://en.wikipedia.org/wiki/Porter_five_forces_analysis

8 Future of Planning a Conversation, Admap February 2010; see [Online] http://www.geniussteals.co/wp-content/uploads/2013/05/Choose-the-Future-Faris-Yakob-AdMap.pdf

9 Heath, Robert and Fieldwich, Paul (2007) [accessed 25 November 2014] 50 Years Using the Wrong Model of TV Advertising [Online] http://www.bath.ac.uk/management/research/pdf/2007-03.pdf

10 Wegner, Daniel M (February 2003) [accessed 25 November 2014] The Mind's Best Trick – How We Experience Conscious Will [Online] http://www.wjh.harvard.edu/~wegner/pdfs/trick.pdf

11 Heath, Robert and Fieldwich, Paul (2007) [accessed 25 November 2014] 50 Years Using the Wrong Model of TV Advertising [Online] http://www.bath.ac.uk/management/research/pdf/2007-03.pdf

12 118 118 – Got Your Number! (4 October 2012) [accessed 25 November 2014] [Online] https://www.youtube.com/watch?v=qx2viPxfoig

13 Budweiser (4 October 2006) [accessed 25 November 2014] Budweiser Wassup [Online] https://www.youtube.com/watch?v=W16qzZ7J5YQ

14 One of the most viewed was the Superfriends spoof (27 July 2008) [accessed 25 November 2014] Superfriends Spoof [Online] https://www.youtube.com/watch?v=Py2g74nOJPU

15 Zimmer, Carl (13 December 2005) [accessed 25 November 2014] Children Learn by Monkey See, Monkey Do. Chimps Don't [Online] http://www.nytimes.com/2005/12/13/science/13essa.html

16 Dandad.org [accessed 25 November 2014] Lynx Pulse Case Study [Online] http://www.dandad.org/en/lynx-pulse/

17 Parr, Ben (10 January 2011) [accessed 25 November 2014] Twitter's New CEO Finally Nails Down the Company's Long-Term Vision [Online] http://mashable.com/2011/01/10/twitters-new-ceo-finally-nails-down-the-companys-long-term-vision/

18 This further evolved to include rented media when it became clear that you did not own your Facebook profile, but a satisfying acronym has yet to be coined

19 Jenkins, Henry (6 November 2006) [accessed 25 November 2014] Eight Traits of the Emerging Media Landscape [Online] http://henryjenkins.org/2006/11/eight_traits_of_the_new_media.html

20 McCracken, Grant, *Chief Culture Officer*, Basic Books; first trade paper edition (10 May 2011)

21 Baer, Jeff [accessed 25 November 2014] 70% of Companies Ignore Customer Complaints on Twitter [Online] http://www.convinceandconvert.com/social-media-monitoring/70-of-companies-ignore-customer-complaints-on-twitter/

22 Jarvis, Jeff (1 February 2012) [accessed 25 November 2014] Facebook Goes Public: Zuckerberg in Public Parts & WWGD? [Online] http://buzzmachine.com/2012/02/01/facebook-goes-public-zuckerberg-in-public-parts-wwgd/

23 Jenkins, Henry (12 December 2006) [accessed 25 November 2014] How Transmedia Storytelling Begat Transmedia Planning... (Part Two) [Online] http://henryjenkins.org/2006/12/how_transmedia_storytelling_be_1.html

24 Theguardian.com [accessed 25 November 2014] 5 Social Media Lessons to Learn From Ford, *Guardian* [Online] http://www.theguardian.com/salesforce-partner-zone/5-social-media-lessons-to-learn-from-ford

25 IACP Center For Social Media [accessed 25 November 2014] Fun Facts [Online] http://www.iacpsocialmedia.org/Resources/FunFacts.aspx

26 Percolate [Online] www.percolate.com

27 Richards, Ben and Yakob, Faris (24 August 2006) [accessed 25 November 2014] Fill Up Your Advertool Kit [Online] http://www.mediapost.com/publications/article/47199/the-new-next-fill-up-your-advertool-kit.html

28 Brian [accessed 25 November 2014] An Open Letter To All Of Advertising And Marketing [Online] http://2.bp.blogspot.com/_QjhMFKRvyqo/TGmCVBlyB5I/30AAADSA/4cM57HC302c/s1600/letter.jpg

29 Baskin, Merry (2010) [accessed 25 November 2014] The Future of Planning – ADMAP Planners Roundtable: Six planning sages debate the future of their discipline. With Will Collin, Rachel Hatton, Adam Morgan, John Owen and Sarah Watson [Online] https://www.econbiz.de/Record/future-planning-admap-planners-roundtable-

future-planning-planning-sages-debate-future-discipline-with-will-
collin-rachel-hatton-adam-morgan-john-owen/10008381059

Chapter 11

1 Gilbert, D (2007) *Stumbling on Happiness*, p 4, Vintage, UK

2 Dennett, D (1992) *Consciousness Explained*, Back Bay Books; 1st edition, USA

3 Greelish, David (2 April 2013) [accessed 25 November 2014] An Interview with Computing Pioneer Alan Kay [Online] http://techland.time.com/2013/04/02/an-interview-with-computing-pioneer-alan-kay/

4 Baylis, Chris (20 December 2011) [accessed 25 November 2014] Don't Create An Ad, Create A World... [Online] http://ihaveanidea.org/articles/2011/12/20/don%E2%80%99t-create-an-ad-create-a-world%E2%80%A6/

5 Old Spice (4 February 2010) [accessed 25 November 2014] Old Spice: The Man Your Man Could Smell Like [Online] https://www.youtube.com/watch?v=owGykVbfgUE

6 Wieden+Kennedy (14 July 2010) [accessed 25 November 2014] Old Spice, Digital Response [Online] http://www.wk.com/campaign/digital_response

7 Wasserman, Todd (29 March 2011) [accessed 25 November 2014] Kraft Mac & Cheese Ad Based on Consumer's Tweet Runs on Conan [VIDEO] [Online] http://mashable.com/2011/03/29/kraft-mac-cheese-ad-conan/

8 Collins, Scott (14 September 2009) [accessed 25 November 2014] The former late-night king returns with a relatively low-cost alternative to scripted prime-time fare – and that has some job-jittery industry folks hoping the network's programming experiment fails [Online] http://articles.latimes.com/2009/sep/14/entertainment/et-leno14

9 Stelter, Brian (20 February 2011) [accessed 25 November 2014] TV Industry Taps Social Media to Keep Viewers' Attention [Online] http://www.nytimes.com/2011/02/21/business/media/21watercooler.html

10 Yakob, Rosie (7 January 2013) [accessed 25 November 2014] 5 Social TV Truths [Online] http://www.digiday.com/publishers/5-truths-about-social-tv/

11 Ibid

12 Ibid

13 Pollard, Mark (14 October 2010) [accessed 25 November 2014] How To Do Account Planning – A Simple Approach [Online] http://www.markpollard.net/how-to-do-account-planning-a-simple-approach/

14 Blooberg.com (1 August 2004) [accessed 25 November 2014] Online Extra: Jeff Bezos on Word-of-Mouth Power [Online] http://www.businessweek.com/stories/2004-08-01/online-extra-jeff-bezos-on-word-of-mouth-power

15 Kay, Gareth (23 July 2009) [accessed 25 November 2014] We Need a New Idea About Ideas [Online] http://www.slideshare.net/garethk/we-need-a-new-idea-about-ideas

16 Henry, Steve (27 March 2012) [accessed 25 November 2014] Snake Oil [Online] http://stevehenry.campaignlive.co.uk/2012/05/27/snake-oil/

17 Vanderbilt, Tom (22 September 2008) [accessed 25 November 2014] Mitchell Joachim: Redesign Cities From Scratch [Online] http://www.wired.com/politics/law/magazine/16-10/sl_joachim

18 Adamson, Allen (25 April 2001) [accessed 25 November 2014] Volkswagen, BMW Understand What It Takes to Stand Out [Online] http://www.forbes.com/sites/allenadamson/2011/04/25/volkswagen-and-bmw-understand-it-takes-a-compelling-story-not-numbers-to-stand-out-on-the-lot/

Epilogue

1 Negroponte, N (1995) *Being Digital*, Alfred A Knopf, Inc, USA

FURTHER READING

Books

Armstrong, K (2006) *A Short History of Myth*, Canongate US, first trade paper edition, UK

Ball, P (2004) *Critical Mass*, Gottfried Achenwall, UK

Baudrillard, J (2010) *America*, Verso, new edition, USA

Dennett, D (1991) *Consciousness Explained*, Little, Brown and Co, USA

Dru, J-M (2007) *How Disruption Brought Order*, Palgrave Macmillan Trade, UK

Earls, M (2009) *Herd*, John Wiley & Sons, first updated edition, USA

Eliot, TS (1920) *The Sacred Wood: Essays on poetry and criticism*, Dodo Press (2009), USA

Feldwick, P (2002) *What is Brand Equity, Anyway?*, NTC Publications, UK

Fox, K (2004) *Watching the English*, Nicholas Brealey America, second edition (2014), UK

Gilbert, D (2006) *Stumbling on Happiness*, Knopf, USA

Gladwell, M (2000) *The Tipping Point*, Little, Brown, USA

Gladwell, M (2007) *Blink*, Back Bay Books, USA

Gleick, J (2011) *The Information*, Pantheon Books, USA; Fourth Estate, UK

Godin, S (1999) *Permission Marketing*, Simon & Schuster, USA

Grant, J (2000) *The New Marketing Manifesto*, Texere Publishing, new edition, UK

Graves, P (2010) *Consumer.ology*, Nicholas Brealey Publishing, UK

Heath, D and Heath, C (2007) *Made to Stick*, Random House, USA

Heath, R (2001) *The Hidden Power of Advertising*, NTC Publications, UK

Heath, R (2012) *Seducing the Subconscious: The psychology of emotional influence in advertising*, Wiley-Blackwell, UK

James, W (1890) *The Principles of Psychology*, Macmillan and Co Ltd, UK

Jenkins, H (2006) *Convergence Culture*, New York University Press, USA

Jenkins, H (2013) *Spreadable Media*, NYU Press, USA

Johnson, S (2011) *Where Good Ideas Come From*, Riverhead Trade, reprint edition, USA

Kahneman, D (2011) *Thinking Fast and Slow*, Farrar, Straus and Giroux, USA

Klein, N (1999) *No Logo*, Knopf, Canada

Lehrer, J (2009) *How We Decide*, Mariner Books, reprint edition, USA

Levitt, S and and Dubner, S (2005) *Freakonomics*, William Morrow, USA

Macknik, S, Martinez-Conde, S and Blakeslee, S (2011) *Sleights of Mind: What the neuroscience of magic reveals about our everyday deceptions*, Picador, reprint edition, UK

McCracken, G (2009) *Chief Culture Officer*, Basic Books, first trade paper edition (2011) USA

McCracken, G (2012) *Culturematic*, Harvard Business Review Press, USA

Morgan, A (2009) *Eating the Big Fish*, Wiley, UK, USA

Ogilvy, D (1985) *Ogilvy on Advertising*, Vintage, USA

Pavitt, J (2014) *Brand New*, V&A Publishing, new edition, UK

Pine, J and Gilmore, J (2011) *The Experience Economy*, Harvard Business Review Press, USA

Schacter, D (1996) *Searching For Memory*, Basic Books, USA

Schwartz, B (2004) *The Paradox of Choice*, Harper Perennial, USA

Shirky, C (2010) *Cognitive Surplus: How technology makes consumers into collaborators*, Penguin Group, USA

Stephenson, N (1995) *The Diamond Age*, Bantam Spectra, USA

Thaler, R and Sunstein, C (2008) *Nudge*, Yale University Press, USA

Warhol, A (1975) *The Philosophy of Andy Warhol (From A to B and Back Again)* Harvest, USA

Watts, D (2012) *Everything is Obvious Once You Know the Answer*, Crown Business, USA

Wolf, M (2003) *The Entertainment Economy*, Crown Business, USA

Papers

Binet, Les and Field, Peter (June 2009) [accessed 25 November 2014] Empirical Generalisations about Advertising Campaign Success [Online] http://farisyakob.typepad.com/files/binet-field-ipa-databank-empirical-generalizations-about-advertising-campaign-success.pdf

Bullmore, Jeremy (2002) [accessed 25 November 2014] Posh Spice & Persil: The Value of Fame [Online] http://www.wpp.com/wpp/marketing/branding/articles-poshspice/

Feldwick, Paul [accessed 25 November 2014] Exploding the Message Myth [Online] http://www.thinkbox.tv/server/show/nav.1015

Glasgow, RDV (1995) Madness, Masks, and Laughter: An essay on comedy, Fairleigh Dickinson University Press, USA

Jenkins, Henry (6 November 2006) [accessed 25 November 2014] Eight Traits of the Emerging Media Landscape [Online] http://henryjenkins.org/2006/11/eight_traits_of_the_new_media.html

Kirby, Alan (2006) [accessed 25 November 2014] The Death of Postmodernism and Beyond [Online] https://philosophynow.org/issues/58/The_Death_of_Postmodernism_And_Beyond

Klages, M [accessed 25 November 2014] Claude Levi-Strauss: The Structural Study of Myth [Online] http://www.colorado.edu/English/ENGL2012Klages/levi-strauss.html

Lethem, Jonathan (February 2007) [accessed 25 November 2014] The Ecstasy of Influence: A Plagiarism [Online] http://www.sunydutchess.edu/faculty/allen/lethem%20-%20ecstasy%20of%20influence.pdf

Levitt, Theodore (July 2004) [accessed 25 November 2014] Marketing Myopia, *Harvard Business Review* [Online] https://hbr.org/2004/07/marketing-myopia/ar/1

Wegner, Daniel M (February 2003) [accessed 25 November 2014] The Mind's Best Trick – How We Experience Conscious Will [Online] http://www.wjh.harvard.edu/~wegner/pdfs/trick.pdf

Resources

The World Advertising Research Council (WARC) hosts all the IPA Effectiveness award papers – and lots of other research besides

INDEX

Note: page numbers in *italics* indicate Figures.

CPSIA information can be obtained
at www.ICGtesting.com
Printed in the USA
BVHW01s2335150118
505283BV00019B/1081/P